1

We-be 'G' Angels

By Netanis Lopez

2019,2020 ©
Revised 2016, 2017, 2018
ISBN 978 – 0 – 359 – 19860 – 3
Lulu Press. Inc.

Reader's Prayer

Dear God,

May all who read and/or comes across this book:

May it bless them, as they relate to it.

May it touch the hearts of the untouchable. May it reach the unreachable and

May it teach the unteachable.

May they come to understand that Christ has already forgiven you like He has forgiven me. And It is never too late to change your life around. It is my best intention to inspire, help others believe by the proof of my life, from being transformed from a wretched person to a believer of how God has saved me. If He can do it for me, He can certainly do it for you too. By the love that God has invested in me, May you find peace, understanding, purpose and meaning within yourself.

Amen.

For: Neiona, Sheiona, Frederick, Jamale, Dawn, Tim & Tonya, Amin, Tyra, Edie, Rusty, Chase, Kara, Tai, Cc, Robin and daughter, Vince, Torre Lynn, Megan, Liz, The Rachel Bey Family, Rick, Jessie, BeFrank, Rosa R, Rosi, The Unroe's, Mandy D, Michelle C, The Mangos, Audra H, Fátima & her children, Audra Z, Butterfly, Tammy J, Lydia, Ashley J, Ty, Paul D, Sue, Jazmyn, Tam, Aunt Freda, Annie Mae, Crystal, Donna R, Mary Mac, Trina P, Aretha Van Horn, Stephanie B, Roberta K, Monica R, Mimi C, Gennetta M, Colette G & sisters, Shequarius P, Ms. Ginny, Kelly H, Jaimey V, Kizzy, The Dooley's, Jason Z, Alana, Tony T, Nicole A, Lillian E - S, Jamilla B, Cynthia M, Rochelle F, Janet F, Sandra M, Jill & Joy, Brooke S, Amy T, Danielle B, Bianca R, Steve C, Chris S, Jan B, Jan S, Yolonda, Shannon, Mr.& Mrs. H.J. Jackson, Carmen, Ms. Marti, Dannetta B, Amberlyn Monique, Jesús, Kristina, Tasha, Wilbur Jr, Ms. Ann, Edna G, Lori & family, Grandma Martha, Chanel, Sheri, Joseph G. Ballard, John B, John M, Ms. Gloria, Rosie, The Pitts Family, Ms. Lashunda, Amy D, Denise D, Raul & Cindy Cendo, Reggie B, Ashely G, Amanda C, Keida, Tiny, Aretha Van Horn, Stephanie B, Trina P, Nicole C, Vivian M, Brandon G, Rita C, Lynnette C, Melinda S, Michelle R, Victoria G, Shannon B, The Sharp's, The Lopez's, The Wilmer's, Ainalen R, Robert H, Denise & Clara, Audrey N, Rebecca, Ms,Erika, Michelle D, Ms. Merritt, Anna V, Marco Cruz, Geneva K, Gerald W, Marion G, Chantel B, The Godfrey's, The Callihan's, The Women of Abuse, Chemical & Codependency Classes, Heather C, Bob E, Jodine and family.

Dedicated:

To God, to myself, my mother, my only sister Néna, my brother Peto, my grandmother, for my children, and their children's children and anyone else that this book can relate to.

Special Dedication:

To my junior high school friend Nettie. I dedicate this to you.
We both have suffered broken hearts of love from a man we
thought we'd spend the rest of our life with. We both used to excess
of substance abuse. Different times, different ways, but our endings
were the same. We both used to numb the pain of our feelings so we
couldn't feel the broken heartedness of our emotions. This is also dedicated
to anybody else who has ever suffered from a broken heart, from unhealthy
relationships, first loves, and divorces.

Front Book Cover:

By Bianca Russell,
Artist & Painter
"The First Joel" 2017

Special Shout-Out:

To Christa Lynn, Founder of ITJ-
Into The Jordan –
All the leaders and the ladies past &present
in group. –
Thank you for all
your inspiration, listening
and patience with me.
My famous words:
"My book's almost done."
Ms. Joann – Timeline -
It set me in the right direction.
Ms. Sharon – For encouraging me.
Ms. Mandie – Always a kind word to say…

Special Extra Thanks:

Dawn – Typist / sister/friends thru Christ
Carmen Perez - Computer Tech / friends thru Christ

To my friend that typed this up at the libraries and my other friend that took time out of her Saturday mornings to make sure this book got printed. I thank them both for their patience with me and the changing of my mind. Lol.
For where two or three are gathered in my name, there am I among them." Matthew 18:20 ESV For this is the truth as we all stayed praying, before, during and after, it was God that brought this all together in His name till the very ending of this book.

There is nothing that is impossible, with God everything is possible. So, what we heard in West Virginia, in a small back woods church, The House of Prayer: Pastor Yvettea Wilmer: *'Him – Possible.' With Him, everything is possible…I learned that day, not impossible but to say 'Him-Possible.'*

But Jesus looked at them and said to them, "With men this is impossible, but with God all things are possible." Matthew 19:26 NKJV

Introduction:

The story you are about to read contains *street lingo, street talk,* and words that are spelled according to how one would talk being in the streets. What I call *'skrate from da botm'.* Some words are misspelled on purpose. My nickname for instance. "Tina" derived from my baby name 'Teeny. When I moved to Florida in 1984 nobody could pronounce Netanis. That had always been a problem for me. So I would say my name is Teeny and they would reply, "Okay Tina." Basically, that's how I got the name and I took it to the next level and it became my stage name. I danced by in the clubs. Adding on "we-be" was later adapted due to more than one Tina in the club. And of course the way I talked I always would saying, *"I be doing this and I be doing doing that,"* so they started calling me "we-be tina." That later became my street name. There was no confusion who you were talking about because I was the only one with that strange name. Today I no longer wish to shut the door on that name. I turn it around to the positive and use it as my stage name when I do my poetry at open mic night, as you will continue to read about.

This book was never supposed to be my life story. As it turned out, that's what ended up happening. It was just supposed to be a book of finished poems and short background stories of how they came and my unfortunate situations that led to it. This is how I was inspired to write the poems. But it seemed like the more I got into the backgrounds of my inspiration, the deeper I dug into my past of pain   the longer the backgrounds seemed to get. It was only by the grace of God that I gained the courage to keep on writing and this has become my way of healing and bringing all my baggage to the light. Writing has become my therapeutic healing for me; It always has and I believe to this day, it always will be. I will not apologize for the way I talked, for that was how it was coming from the "botm' I endured many encounters being brought up from Camden, NJ all the way from the adult clubs of West Palm Beach to the streets of West Palm and how I survived, by writing. I guess you could call me a poet. But my goal is to write, inspire and share what has taken me over 45 plus years to achieve of what God has done for me. This book goes out to all the ones caught up in *'the struggle'* of life. And especially to the ones that never got a chance to know God and who *Jesus Christ* is; the role He's played in this world from the very beginning of time. Also to get to know him and what He is capable of doing in modern day miracles to help them recover. For the ones that never made it out and how 'bout the 'innocent ones' who was born without that choice, starting with my grandson Joel.

Some names, dates and places have been changed to protect the innocent private lives. This book may contain graphic descriptions and may not be suitable for a younger audience. If you're younger than 18, just make sure an adult approves the material you are about to read. Thank you for continuing on reading. May you enjoy the book and hope you can gain insight and not judgement about "the other side of the tracks." This book is suitable for hospitals, jails, prisons, and other institutions regardless of race, religion, or origin.

The actual order of this book is of years from 2003-2017, when I wrote my first poem again. I backed it up from 1966, the year I was born, since that's when my actual story does take place. So I guess what they say is true that everyone has a story and the story starts at home.

Front Cover Story: "The First Joel"

About the painting on the cover: It is of a baby in a diaper, reading a book, with the look of confidence and not surprise. The baby is looking as the artist paints. He stays very still, *posing perfectly propped*. Smart is he, I believe; for he knows something we don't at this moment. As the artist, Bianca continues to paint, the baby knows the day is coming when this painting will go to someone that hurts and loves deeply; as if, the painter has felt the same emotions. With every stroke of her brush, with acrylics of most *divine* colors, confidently waiting for the day the painting goes home with love, taking all their pain away, as everyone finds comfort and peace…as all remains well with their souls.

"Most Mysterious Ways"

I never met Bianca before I purchased this painting at an event called Speak My Peace, put on by GCL, Gulf Coast Leisure of Fort Myers (a networking company) founder Marco Cruz and hosted by BeFrank It's for local artists to express themselves by poetry, song, painting, storytelling and dance or any form of talent. The event is held the first Saturday of the month, in the evening from 8pm – 11pm. I spoke my poetry that is contained in the book, as I entered it. You could say it was healing therapy for myself. That's where I also met Bianca.

A particular Saturday in the spring, I went out for one of my walks with God, like I always do before the evening event. I guess you can say I was feeling melancholy, bereaving while thinking of my grandson. I began to tear up as I thought of my grandson Joel and my unfinished book. I began to pray. *"Lord, I am missing him today. Could you just let me see him so I know once again he's straight?"* Quickly I recanted my request, thinking it was so unheard of. I apologized to God for a demand of such a silly request. For I knew it was impossible to see him today. By God, we hadn't had a service for him yet, much less picked up the ashes. That evening at Speak My Peace, as the evening was coming to a close, was when I spotted the picture and met Bianca. I could not take my eyes off the painting. They were fixed on it. I was in *awe*. I'm looking right at my grandson. I was speechless for a moment. As I spoke of my grandson with both of our eyes watering, I knew that she knew, as she asked me for a hug. See, there's nothing that is impossible when it comes to the Lord and how He works. To me, when God shows up, you can best believe with a guarantee that He will show out. My silly prayer was answered. I got to see my grandson Joel as I believe he lives in Heaven. Little did we know that Bianca's painting that I purchased that night would be the front cover with her permission she allowed me to name it and use it. You don't have to convince me how God works in the *most mysterious ways.*

Updated October 2020
Revised Edition 10

Broken Wings

December 2016

"One fine March day, just before spring,
God sent an angel,
Angel with broken wings.
But why would he send him to us and
- broken of all things?"

I didn't understand this;
This baby angel,
Of pure and true;
Couldn't figure it out,
Didn't have a clue.
Yet, I know not to question God... Yet...
Still... I don't know what we gonna do.
So, I did what came natural
From the realms of my heart,
To love this baby boy,
It was a beginning and a start.
So to name him must be special...
So I thought......... hmm.........
'bout the baby Jesus, the very 1st Christmas,
And how the Angels sang "The First Noel."
And we started with a name of Love,
And named him...... Joel.

By: Netanis Lopez

We-be 'G' Angels
My Walk with God

If you want to know the end, look at the beginning.
                              – African proverb

NOTE TO READER:

After seven revised editions of this book, many mistakes were made, mostly on my behalf. On this present day in January 2020. I am pleased with myself because I did my best to my ability. Like it says in the Word: **Ecclesiastics 9:10 Whatever work you do, do your best.**

Forward

The 4 poems you are about to read are about the wind blowing, me walking, and God speaking to me. While walking to the store, I was thinking about my life and all my struggles. This book I am writing was supposed to be only poems. Then I thought, "Wait a minute. These background stories are getting longer and longer. I have to explain more." So I closed my eyes and stood still and prayed. And I listened. And this is what God revealed to me:

January 22, 2017

Listen to the Wind

Listening to the wind
As it blows thru my ears.
I have heard the sound
For many years.

Listening to the wind
Sounding like thunder.
In a sea shell … the wind?
Where does it come from?
Who makes it?
I wander - & wonder.

Listening to the wind,
As it drys my tears
It wisked away all my fears.
Takes away my pain of yesterday
Makes me wanna stop & pause & pray,
Makes me wanna
Thank God,
For today.
By Netanis Lopez.

Calling Out My Name

Opening the window,
*   A gush of wind blew in.*
As trees stirred
*   my mind whirled,*
My tears dried
*   That I cried.*
Exhaling, I sighed.
Smiling at the marvelous
*   gush of the wind.*
Blowing away all my sins
Coulda swore I heard
*   a voice,*
And God calling out my
*   name.*
As God spoke, He said,
*   "Well done, Well done...Netanis Lopez!"*

After writing this I felt so proud of myself. I had begun to learn how to listen for His guidance. It was then I began to realize I am a child of God. I felt His presence and realized this book had to be more than just poems. There was so much more to my story of my past history. With each thought it led to another and another and I knew I just had to write more. I just didn't know where to start. Later that very same day, when I went for my usual walks with God, it was revealed to me. I had gotten so excited and proud of myself for my obedience of being still and listening to Our Savior.

I think about now of the many times the Lord saved me from death and that is real, true, deep love. I knew He had a purpose for my life! And that is why I share my whole story, the good and the bad. Most of all, I knew God loved me no matter what. And this kind of love, I never deserved.

WOW!!! Love? Me? I started recognizing myself. I love, love. I have always thought to this day that He had installed this power in me and I wanted to exercise this wonderful gift of not just writing, but of loving others too. I wanted to teach others to love themselves by my example. Coming to love and respect myself was a process of elimination of my defective desires and wants. I had to put God first by a simple prayer. In the Bible verse *But seek ye first the kingdom of God, and his righteousness; and all these things shall be added unto you. KJB Matthew 6:33.* From experience of being exhausted of my past, I always did things my way. And for some strange reason, it never quite worked out. It's important for me to always read my devotions first, write my take of it and apply it throughout my day. Because I know I am nothing without Him, my greatest desire is to seek Him daily and stay in constant prayer and meditation about everything. I always run everything by God before I make a decision.

January 25, 2017

<u>Greatest Power</u>

*"Going to the beach
I did, now I'm back
I wrote and thinked
on a small hand towel
I sat.
It's the next day
And another chapter of
   this book takes place
Nice to figure out,
My life wasn't a waste."*

*If I never wrote no more,
It would be alright with me.
But God has instilled me with
His gifts, He showers,
   me with LOVE,
The Greatest of all,
The Greatest power.*

*Showers me with words
hour after hour.
Still the best He ever
gave me is, LOVE
The Greatest Power.*

*I will pass it on to my
daughters and sons.
And I know which part
I will be giving,
It's stated in my will
My will of the living.*

*They can pass my legacy
on to their grands
And upcoming generations
   of how their grandmother
survived all her trials and
   tribulations.*

                    Netanis Lopez

I was so tired of our family repeating the same mistakes over and over again. I want better for my family. Since I don't have no money to leave them when I die, all I have left is my experiences of where my strength comes from and how my faith has grown through Christ. After all I am just a sinner saved by grace, hope and mercy along with the faith and His love and how God restored me. With all the proof to back it up, I leave them behind my parental legacy, my story.

"My expectations of myself is descended from generations of afflictions and addictions, cycles, repeating over and over. Again, and again. This continues to invade, to pierce my mind, into complete turmoil, into total devastation. But not anymore. With God, the Trinity, three in one. - I stay defeated."

Stop The Ball

Finally,
    I caught the ball-
    from going down the steps.

Since,
    I stopped it,
    I lift the bar,
    set the stage,
    changed the mess
    Got rid of resentment-
    And rage.
    To continue on,
    the struggle

I THINK NOT!!!
    For its been going on too long,
    Too many years,
    So many countless tears.
    This must stop immediately.
    Stop making a wreck.

So I stop't the ball,
    stopped the ball,
        from bouncing
            down the steps.

Netanis Lopez.

Who
am I?

In the beginning the Word already existed. The Word was with God, and the Word was God. He existed in the beginning with God. God created everything through Him, and nothing was created except through Him. The Word gave life to everything that was created, and His life brought light to everyone. The light shines through darkness, and the darkness can never extinguish it.

John 1:1-5 NLT

Chapt. 1 - The Beginning

Long after Adam and Eve, Our Creator of all made another one of his great masterpieces, and that was me, Netanis Jane Lopez, otherwise known as 'Morningstar," it's Indian for Netanis. My middle name Jane means in English, "Gracious and merciful" and in Hebrew it means "Gift from God." It wasn't till I started writing this book that I realized God thought I was worth saving more times than I'd like to remember. Like in the **Psalms 139:16 NIV. Your eyes saw my unformed body; all the days were written in your book before one of them came to be.** Today that day has came to be. I have come to understand a question that went unanswered for many years. *Why me?*

God's grace and mercy had always been with me. God knew what my name was going to be, before my mother named me that because in **Isaiah 49:16, it says, "See, I have written your name on the palms of my hands... NLT.** Today I realize how blessed I really am. What matters to me now was how far I come from what I used to be. I've come to realize today what my calling is thus far. And if you ask me, every living creature has one unique, special purpose like no other one. **Romans 12:6 In his grace, God has given us different gifts for doing certain things well. So if God has given you the ability to prophesy ...do it with as much faith as God has given you.** One of my gifted callings, is to write my experience and share with others, to let them know they can overcome any obstacles that life throws at you, no matter what. I'm living proof. This book is for all people who have hang ups, got hurts from losing love ones and the still sick and suffering people that are still out there. And the babies that are born to the disease of addiction but didn't ask to be here. For no one is perfect. The last time I checked there was only one person I knew of that was perfect and that was Jesus Christ. This is my story of how I moved out of my own way, by not co-signing my own BS and let God do what I humanly couldn't do for myself. I withheld nothing. I pray, as you feast your eyes on my book, may it move you in ways you never thought possible. Amen - This is my story and I'm sticking to it.

As for me, it started in 1966, the year I was born. I was born in Camden, New Jersey, home of the Campbell Soup Company. It was also considered one of the worst, most dangerous city in America. You name it and it probably happened here. Thank God my mother would move us out the city before things got really bad for me. The year was 1972. We moved to Jacksonville, Florida. I was so glad to be moving away for my own reasons. I had been molested since I was about three years old until I was about six, just being fondled. And just before we moved, before my seventh birthday he completely stole my innocence. A new school, a different state, going into the second grade, and a shameful, embarrassing secret. Because he went all the way with me, I would be so different from the new kids because I felt like everybody knew that I had sex. *This is only suppose to happen between grown ups and for people that married.* I thought!

There was only one other person that knew of this at the time, my grandmother. At the time I knew I had to deal with this and tell somebody at such a young age so that's what I did before moving.

So eventually I told my grandmother what my uncle did to me. He had been touching me since my mom and father separated. I understood what rape really meant. My innocence was stolen in a nutshell. I lived in regret and guilt and thought to myself *Who would ever really want me after that?* Sometimes I think for many years. *Why didn't I tell someone sooner?* I was always thinking *it was all my fault* and so I kept my mouth shut. It was my Uncle Wee'am that actually figured it out. He went to pick me up while at my grandmother's house and I jumped in pain, then flinched and began crying. He quickly responded, *"Are you hurt? 'Did somebody hit you? 'Did somebody hurt you?"* I shook my head *yes.* Quickly he said, *"Who?! 'Who did it?!"* He started guessing off names. When he got to my other uncle's name, I shook and shrieked hysterically. It was then he called my grandmother and told her what happened.

She was furious. She picked me up in her arms. She told me she was sorry for what happened and promised me she would see to it that it would never happen again, and it never did. That night I slept with my grandmother and she held me close all night long. I felt so secure and safe as she sang *Jesus Loves Me* to me. I understood the severity of it all and I knew what he did was wrong. The wrongdoings that happened to me should have never taken place.

I carried this with me along with terrible nightmares of unforgettable memories for the next forty-five plus years of my life. I never saw him again until I was 35, sitting at my mother's kitchen table in North Carolina. When I walked in, I was floored. She didn't even tell me he would be there. I couldn't believe my mom had this pervert at her table after everything he did to me! The pain was still fresh and the reality of what actually happened to me surfaced again. I thought I was over all that. I thought I had already forgiven him. But if I did, I took it back the moment I laid eyes on him. He couldn't even look me in the face. I remember I was mad as hell. All my friends that I worked with in the clubs didn't even know that I held a terrible secret. It was because I was still ashamed of myself and embarrassed. One good thing I knew that came out of this and it wasn't hard to figure out, *is what men liked. I knew that by dancing in the clubs, I would get them back. (And I did but that's* another story.) A feeling of more resentments that also came along with the hatred of men. All they ever did was hurt me and leave me. I even refused to wear a *crucifix* at that dark point in my life because it has a man on it.

My mother and father both worked at the factory, Campbell Soup. My father was a supervisor and she worked on the line belt for the labels. He worked a lot of late hours and my mom took care of us. I being the baby of the three kids, got more attention from my father. He favored me and I loved him then and I still do very much until this day. My mom doesn't like his name mentioned. She played the father role while I was growing up. She never let us forget that she was our mother and father. On Father's Day when I was younger, in school when we had to make cards for our dads, I would make one thinking about my father, wishing I could give it to him personally and see him one more time. I would end up giving the card to my mother and that's how the rest of Father's Days to come played out until my late teenage years before I became a young woman.

One of my first memories of my babyhood was violent. Domestic violence is what they call it today. Sadly, for me that was normal in our household. My father came home from work and was physically fighting with my mother. I started screaming. I remember I was eating spaghetti in an old metal high chair and was accidentally knocked out of the chair, hitting the top part of my head, splitting it wide open. His reasoning was that there wasn't enough salt in the spaghetti. It's funny how our past catches up with us. It explains today why I don't care for spaghetti. I needed stitches and no; I didn't get any but my mom cleaned me up. I remember I tasted my own blood because I surely knew this wasn't the taste of spaghetti that my mom made. I still wear that scar till this day. I remember the warmth of my blood running down my face. That sense of my blood soothed me. In the years to come the feeling of what my own blood felt like and tasted like would be my own motivation of my reasoning why I must remain alive. For this would not be the last time I tasted my own blood. This was just the first of many battles in my life to come.

In 1972 Hurricane Agnes came. It was the first storm of the season and we had our own storm to deal with. Papi would be storming home soon. My mother was always telling us she wanted to leave him one day. What we did not expect was it to be so soon. So the night of the big storm, he came home pissed off from work. Mother said to us, "If Papi starts his *shit* tonight, be prepared to go." She knew him well because he started his usual stuff on a Friday night after he got paid. He would usually stop at the bar and have a couple. He would fight with her because he came home broke after gambling on the horses and demand my mother give him money. She told him. "No," and that was enough to set him off and by this time she had enough.

We left right out in the middle of the wind and rain. What a memory! I'll never forget how the wind blew dirt in my eyes. They stung as if someone threw a mound of sand in my face with great force. It went up my nose, in my mouth and pierced my cheeks as if it went straight through my bones.

We stayed with my grandmother for about a month until my mother could devise a plan to figure out what we would do next. We ended up moving on the other side of Camden, until my father's friend spotted my mother and informed him about where we were living. My mom quickly gave away and sold what we couldn't take and we hurriedly left for Jacksonville, Fl. I think back now how God's grace was even there for my mom because we actually moved on *a wing and a prayer*. I finished out the rest of that school year in the second grade in a new school in a new state. That same fiscal year of 1972-73, I would be in the third grade.

Growing up I really never felt like my mom loved me. I don't even remember as a childhood her telling me so. From being molested as a child, my mother didn't really know what kind of affect that would have on me for the next forty-five years or so on my life. Today I take that experience that held me captive most my life and I turned it around for my good. I don't let it bother me anymore. In fact, I'm glad it happened. That has molded me into the person that I am today. It has made me stronger than ever with a great understanding of forgiveness which I think is truly a gift from God. For I know what it's like for a child of five or six to have the innocent stripped away from them without a choice. Back then when I was growing up you didn't talk about stuff like that. I was taught

23

that you could start a whole lot of trouble about your family.   I used to think, *No one is going to believe me anyway.* Also I would be known as a *trouble maker.*

Later I held a resentment against my mom for leaving my father. I thought, *why didn't she try to work this out?* I didn't understand why she couldn't understand me and the way I felt inside. I felt all alone like I was the only one who ever felt like this. Sometimes I would talk back to her and roll my eyes at her. But she never caught me (not till later on in life) and I was relieved because her punishments were harsh but at least I knew my uncle would never touch me again. I understood today why we had to go. She couldn't take the beatings anymore and she wanted a better life for us. No matter what my father did, I still loved him.   I still find great sadness on Father's Day.   For a long time, I had *daddy issues* but thank God today I'm over that. I have a great relationship with my DAD/GOD.   That just sums it all up today as I own my feelings.   I'm powerless what happened to me when I was young. It's today that I can tell my story and let others know they are not alone and I can relate to how they feel. I would like others to know its not your fault.

Chapt. 2 - Discovering God

I was glad to be going to Florida and going into a new school even if it was in "Hot behind" Florida. It was so different here. All the roofs were flat, no basements and no ice freezing snow or cold temperatures compared to Camden. In Florida the only things that troubled me was the baby alligators that crawled around, a.k.a. lizards, Florida's natural habitat. Not to mention the curly tailed lizards that reminded me of dinosaurs. If that wasn't enough, they had bald headed rats that were big as dogs and they called them armadillos. That was the down part of Florida. The upside was that roaring I had never heard before. It was coming through the trees, echoing in my ears. It was a beautiful sound. It brought me peace and tranquility. It also gave me a sense of freedom. Curious as I was being in this new place, I did a little investigation. "I must find out what this sound is." That's what I told myself. I found out it was the beach. And it was so close. A hop, skip, and jump through the woods away.

It was a place where I found serenity and God. The thought came to me. *God is everywhere. He 'dun followed me to Florida.* I fell in love with Him even more, even though I couldn't see Him. Only God could make a place so wonderful to take my pain away. I loved swimming in the water. It was so clear and blue. I could see all the way to the bottom. I could even see the polish on my toes. Here is where I would go to talk to God. Today it's known as Step 11, Meditation. I was doing recovery steps without even knowing it. I guess I always was an addict and today I'm okay with that.

Now the only thing I missed about New Jersey when it came down to it was my grandmother. Now she was the glue that held us to all together. When we left, she cried; I cried. We all cried. I remember sobbing hysterically inside. When the tears didn't spill down my cheeks, only she knew what I was really feeling. She also knew that I was grateful for all she taught me especially keeping that creep member of my family away from me. It was my grandmother that taught me about Jesus. She used to sing the song *Jesus Loves Me* to all us grandkids. She also taught us about the stories in the Bible. She often told me when I'm feeling down and sad, just sing the song *Jesus Loves Me* and I will begin to feel better; that she promised. So in times of trouble, no matter what it is, I still sing the song and her promises were true. I did start to feel better. I just missed her so much. She molded me into the grandmother I am today and I teach my grandkids that same song she so lovingly taught me.

We went back to Camden many times after that, especially Easter and Christmas. That was our family gathering holidays. All of us looked forward every year to going back to see my grandma. My grandmother was a baker and a diabetic. She would always make cookies, chocolate cakes and pies. I really loved her chocolate chip cookies. They were my favorite. Even till this day, if anything has any chocolate in it, you can count me in. I keep her picture by my bedside table. My grandmother, she was my first 'G' when I look back on it now, next to God that is. So the 'G' stands for God first, anyone "God-like" or pertaining to my Grandma or anything that starts with 'G.' Take for instance; grace, glory, gifts, guidance, guard, grief, ghetto, ol'g, gangster, genealogists, genealogy, genetics, "GPS" - Grace's Protection Service, generosity, etc. etc.

We lived in Jacksonville, Florida from 1972-1979. From the 2nd grade all the way till the 8th grade, me and my sister were picked on a lot in school. We were bullied because we were poor. Our shoes and socks always had holes in them. We wore hand-me-downs that my grandmother would send us from the church made out of polyester. Those clothes were so hot. We hated wearing them. My sister and I were so embarrassed because the clothes were so old fashioned. But my mom made us wear them anyway. To evade the harassment from the other classmates we would change in the woods before we got to school and change back before we came home. Life was rough in Jacksonville. There were often times when there wasn't a lot to eat. Sometimes we didn't have electricity. Well 'lot of the times we didn't have electricity. One time just before the summer and while we still had electric, I used to rush home to watch *Gilligan's Island* on our black and white plastic 13-inch T.V (which my mom still has today) I had an out of body experience. I felt my body getting hot and then raise up. A question that went through my mind was, *Is this all the further this world has come since the last time I was here?* I felt as if I had been on this earth before. Perplexed I sought out God for my answers and spent a lot of time at the beach praying. Hoping that things would get better. Although it took a while, God finally answered my prayers.

Today I learn many times how I must wait on the Lord and that He hears my prayers which takes me to the Bible verse: **Psalms 27:14 - Wait on the LORD: be of good courage, and he shall strengthen thine heart: wait, I say, on the LORD.** Yet still on this present day I pray for more patience. Practicing my patience, I strive with desire to do better. So, I wait and wait, listening for the Lord to speak and reveal Himself to me. He usually does on my daily meditational walks with Him. Sometimes God speaks to me through a song or a scripture or even His words will come from a total stranger that doesn't even know my situation but what they said I was thinking of that with some doubt of contemplating was no longer an issue for then I knew what my answer is.

Chapt. 3 - Growing Up
Part 1

My mom got remarried to sailor and in 1979, just after my stepdad got out the Navy, we moved. None of us had a choice in the matter. Not me, my brother nor my sister. We were all told things would be better, a lot better. My mother's husband was okay he liked having a ready- made family so he said. His family was from West Virginia. We moved with high hopes for a better future. We then packed up all our belongings rented a moving truck and left for Wonderful, Wild, Beautiful, White Sulphur Springs West Virginia. What an amazing place to be and live. I couldn't believe we lived here! Wow!! As I looked around in amazement, I couldn't grasp that we actually moved. Mountains every everywhere; God was such in abundance everywhere you looked. No wonder when people ask where you from, they say: I'm from West by God Virginia! West Virginia. What a great place to live. It really was almost heaven. When upon awakening in the morning it was like the clouds came down on the tips of the Blue Ridge Mountains; creating an euphoria of being in Heaven. What an awesome Creator is He!

Things were good for a while. Schools were easier but circumstances didn't change. In junior high school I was still bullied but this time the bullying was different. They didn't pick on me because I was poor, they picked on me because I was pretty. All the boys seemed to give me attention and all the girls hated me for that except for my girlfriend Nettie. She always stuck up for me. She would tell me, "Girl, you new meat." The girls that picked on me kept the pot stirred. Just when the taunting would calm down, another girl would instigate more. Like I said, it's funny cause during my trip to WV last year in 2018, those same girls that picked on and laughed at me took me and my traveling buddy out to lunch. I brought up the subject of being bullied and I relayed to them how much that hurt me. The look in the one girl's eyes, who was the main bully, her eyes said it all. Just for a moment I felt her indirect apology to me. I knew she was sorry. By being in recovery, I knew she made an indirect amends. I later told them a little bit of my story about living in Jacksonville before I came to West Virginia. They were shocked to learn what had happened to me as a very young child.

See I've learned today that you never know what somebody else has gone through. As for me, I was quickly judged and ridiculed. I couldn't understand why these girls picked on me. Out to lunch that day they explained to me I was, "That girl." That means a girl that's pretty, new and that all the boys paid attention to. I was that new kid on the block and I suppose jealousy of too. For today I have learned to forgive them just by thinking of the verse: ***...Father, forgive them; for they know not what they do...Luke 23:34 KJV.*** And just like the Father said, when you hurt others or are nice to others, you are nice to me too. At least that's how I understand the verse. ***"And the King will say,***

27

'I tell you the truth, when you did it to one of the least of these my brothers and sisters, you were doing it to me!' Matthew 25:40 NLT

Our Home
Part 2

We had a huge thirteen room farmhouse. I found my first boyfriend and we dated from the 8th grade until I graduated in 1984. We went to the prom together. I had sex for the first time out of love and I thought I really knew what love was. But what I figured out was I really didn't know very much. I was very naïve. It's like I knew a lot about a little. I didn't know what drugs were. I didn't know what drinking was all about and I remember it was here I got drunk the first time. The only thing I really knew about drinking was, I didn't like it. Who knew that my whole life would be changed by just one instant? Not really being satisfied of how alcohol made me feel, what I didn't know was that in the years to come I would really find out what drug was my choice; the consequences of drugs and the effects it would have on my life.

I studied CNA nursing when I was a senior that year and I excelled very well. My plans were to go live with my aunt, my mom's sister, in West Palm Beach. I was to continue to go on and go to college to become a medical assistant. Well that was my plan. But I didn't stick with it. Because I relied on my own strength and thought I knew it all. I guess you could say I was running on my own free will. My grandmother taught me better than that. I was always told to pray about everything I did first. So that summer in 1984, I moved to West Palm Beach Florida with my aunt. It was here I would go to college and make a career out of my life. I was determined to be somebody. Little did I know that year in 1984, I would meet my son's father in just only a couple weeks after living there.

He was actually my second boyfriend. In a short time (we barely knew each other) we got engaged and were to be married. Quickly after the announcement to our friends I found out that he was cheating on me. It was one of the worst things that ever happened to me in my whole life thus far, besides what my uncle did to me. This stuff only happens in the movies I thought. It really devastated me and my heart was broken and crushed to pieces. I mean this really shattered me in disbelief of a man that I thought I could trust and that I was so in-love with. I couldn't take what life had dished out to me anymore. This was way too much for me to handle. Then out of the blue and without any warning my mind snapped into an oblivion of realties that I could not accept. This leading me in a panic of devastation and I had my first nervous breakdown.

Backing up in college, I had "dibbled and dabbled" with drugs. Nothing really stuck with me until that day I found out I was being cheated on. One day after hanging out with this girl I met in college, I tried for the first-time freebase cocaine. Although it never interested me, my mind was so clear and numb. I liked what it did to me. It seemed to take all my pain away. I mean, I really liked not being able to feel and to hurt no more. As long as I stayed *high* that is. So that's what I did. I was messed up all the time. When I stopped to gain some sense of reality and sleep, I felt so depressed all the thoughts going around my head boggled me. I promised myself I wouldn't do this *stuff* again. But wasn't long after that at age nineteen again, my mind quickly snapped into another nervous breakdown. After I came out of my psychosis which lasted almost two weeks, sickly I went out and bought some more drugs. I just wanted to escape the horrible memories that had plagued me for so many years.

Because I needed money like right now to get more drugs, I asked the same girl that introduced to the drugs, on how to make quick money. She showed me about the adult entertainment biz. I had never even known these kinds of places existed. Like a drug I was hooked instantly. So, I dropped out of college not caring about anything. I continued on this destructive path of getting money and drugs. That's how I got into dancing and ended up going MIA and I wasn't in Miami. But I did end up on the strip in Fort Lauderdale in 1985.

At this time, I was dancing at the clubs and not having no accountability. I was destructive to my own self and I was totally lost. In fact, I was so lost that I didn't even know what day of the week it was. It was like the fairy tale Rip Van Winkle by Washington Irving. It was about a man who fell asleep in the Catskill Mountains for twenty years and missed the American Revolution. Like Rip the last time I checked who the president was it was a guy they say had a peanut farm President Carter; nor did I know what holiday was coming. I figured that out by going to the store and the store being closed reading the sign, "Closed on Christmas." And that's how I knew it was Christmas Day. I knew it was coming because I saw the Christmas lights and decorations.

By this time, my mom had put a missing person report out on me. I found myself alone, confused and hopeless. I cried out to God and asked Him to send me an angel. By this time, I had no choice but to go back home for the first time; I was spiritually bankrupt. I don't know if it was my instincts or common sense but I felt a realm of peace come over me when I thought of home. That sense of relief and   calmness I experienced I know today, was *Divine Intuition* of the Lord. A confirmation, *'It was time to go home'* and so I did.

Little did I know, God had answered my prayer and sent me an angel. By the time I came back home in 1986, I found myself pregnant with my first child. My mother welcomed me back with open arms and not asking too many questions. It brought to my mind the story of the Prodigal Son in the Bible that my grandmother taught me about. I realized that my mom was worried about me and that maybe she does love me. Now I had a reason to get myself straightened out. It was no longer all about me. I was having my own child and I wanted to give my baby the best of me. I wanted to teach him what this world was all about and the things my mother never taught me. I surely didn't want to bring a child into this world without him knowing the facts of life of all the ups and downs this world throws at you.

I left my baby's father, moved in with my mother and worked on myself. I attended therapy sessions and I was told a lot of what I went through in my past and my upbringing had a lot to do with how I felt. This worked for a while. In 1987 my first son was born and then I ended up getting back with his father, the same man that cheated on me. We both agreed to not use again. Since he couldn't keep his part of the bargain to stay clean, I threatened that I would leave him. Just after that and before I knew it, I was pregnant again. I had my second son in 1988. Two weeks after he was born, I left my boys' father for good. I broke up with him for the last time and I never went back to him.

I didn't use anymore when I found out I was pregnant from the first time and I continued to excel and being the woman that I was meant to be. After all this, I still didn't know who I was, wasn't too sure about God anymore, and I didn't know what I wanted to be when I grew up still. All I knew was I just didn't want to use drugs anymore. All I ever wanted was to be married, in love and then live happily ever after, just like in the fairytale books. But the latter of the two never happened.

It's because something was still missing. It's like I had this void in my soul and I tried to explain it to my mom so she could understand what I was feeling but I didn't know how to express the emotions. She told me calmly, *'Honey I think you need to go and talk to somebody'*. I really didn't understand who this *somebody* was, so I dismissed our talk immediately and drew my own conclusion only to realize that I haven't really prayed in a while. I questioned myself. *Had I forgotten about God?* Yes, I had. That night I got down on my knees and prayed. I sobbed like a little child. My hot tears streaming steadily-poured down my puffy, pink cheeks. I don't know much time passed by; all I knew is that I felt a relief of *doubt* leave me. It was like in a long time I felt the presence of God. That night before I went to sleep, I sang *Jesus Love Me* to myself a few times and for the first time since I was little, I didn't cry myself to sleep. I began to want change in my life. Can't believe I was such a disarrayed train wreck at such a young age.

Chapt. 4 - Becoming Responsible

My best friend Nettie that I grew up with, got drunk with and skipped school with in West Virginia moved down here to Florida with me in the summer of 1989. We were always close in our friendship and shared many bonding experiences. One that stands out in my mind was being present for the birth of her first child, a girl. That day she was born I just happened to be training for my CNA certificate and was working on the delivery floor when she had her first daughter. I was a senior in high school. Looking back, that was God making this moment possible from the very beginning for me to be present during my best friend's birth of her first baby. By the time she moved with me in West Palm Beach, she had another daughter by this time. Her second daughter just so happened to be the same age as my first son. Nettie's oldest daughter stayed with her grandmother, Nettie's Mom, so she could start school in the fall, while her youngest daughter accompanied her on her trip down to Florida. She was also going through a bad breakup so we leaned on each other while we teamed up together and proceeded to make it work with our children on board. It was around this time when I met my first husband, both of my daughters' father. It was a hot summer day in July. I remember it very well. I knew one look at him and he would be the man that I would marry. Eventually, I did. My little fairytale was sorta starting to come true. But unexpected circumstances were about to take place.

My aunt who lived two doors down in a duplex and was supposed to watch the kids like she had done so many times in the past, but she at the last minute she wasn't able to. So, the plans Nettie and I had made to go out that night suddenly changed. Instead, she stayed home watching the kids. I ended up proceeding to go out by myself with my other girlfriend. Before I left, Nettie told me she had a strange feeling about going out. I just brushed off and finished getting ready. I assured her I would be extra careful and would return home at a decent hour. We both gave each other a hug. The last thing Nettie said to me before I left was to be *really careful* and *get back safe*. I reassured her that I would be home early and not to worry, just pray. Little did I know in a matter of hours, I would be fighting for my life. However, I didn't know that my life was about to change tragically before I could fulfill the marriage. This same year on September 18, 1989, I was struck by a train in my car.

I had suffered all internal injuries and was bleeding profusely inside. They say I argued with the paramedics because I didn't want to go to the hospital. I was throwing up blood on the side of the car. I was pretty much in bad shape.

The paramedics finally got me on to the stretcher and wheeled me into the hospital emergency room. I heard this voice that I had never heard before. It was telling me, *"It's going to be alright, I got you."* With that confirmation, I closed my eyes, turned my head to the side and I felt blood dripping from my nose and my mouth.

Miami Herald, The (FL)

September 19, 1989

TRAIN HITS CAR

Author: Herald Staff

Edition: PLM BCH
Section: PLM BCH
Page: 1B

Index Terms:
TRAFFIC ACCIDENT RAILROAD PLM BCH

Estimated printed pages: 1

Article Text:

STEVE BRITT / Miami Herald

Tina Lopez, a passenger in a Lincoln that was struck early Monday by a Florida East Coast **train** in Lake Worth, is checked before being taken to St. Mary's Hospital in West Palm Beach. She and the driver.[   ] were listed in critical but stable condition.

Caption:
photo: **Tina Lopez** with rescuers (**ACCIDENT** AUTO FLORIDA), car (s)

I reminded myself of a cat. It felt like I had just got hit by a car, laying on the side of the road and my nose was dripping blood. It was a feeling that I felt before...like the time I fell out the highchair. It was now more than once I tasted my own blood. Yet still it wouldn't be the last. It was also the first time God had spoken to me. A voice that I cannot get confused about and to know that in the future, I would unmistakably recognize and hear His still but firm gentle voice again. I believed it was going to be alright and I'm not going to die because God told me so. At this point in my life, my confidence in that voice had convinced me that for sure I was going to be alright. God's mercy had saved me. I believed I was going to be alright and not to worry so I didn't. In God I put all my trust. The "Unseen," had just saved my life. I never would forget that voice that I've heard a few more times since then.

I was pretty messed up. I had severe internal injuries which included a ruptured spleen and appendix. My liver was torn and my stomach lining got damaged because my ribs were broken. As if that wasn't all, I had four fractures in my back. The doctors had to make an incision from the bottom of my sternum all the way down to my belly button where 21 staples were holding me together. I was even pregnant and didn't know it. The doctors said because the baby was in my tubes, it never passed through. Due to that issue, my left fallopian tube and ovaries were removed. I was later told I would never be able to have any more children. As I came to find out, I would prove all the doctors wrong. This simply was not true. I healed quickly after the accident and a lot of things started changing for me for the better.

My status changed. I had another baby, my first daughter in 1990. I got married in 1991. I had my second daughter in 1994. I was twenty-eight years old. I was back at work, dancing, making good money in the club. Things were going really good. I was making commercials, calendars, postcards; I guess you

32

could say I was being exploited. We all were the strange thing about that is we didn't even know it. The cameramen promised us all copies of the pictures, money and more advertisement. None of that came through. Later we found that some of our pictures were being used for adult magazines and tourists' newspapers as escorting ads. There was really nothing we could do about it.

I was making really decent money. I was taking care of the house. The kids were going to school. I was taking care of my husband, buying cars after cars. I bought gold and jewelry, anything the kids needed but yet, I still wasn't happy. My marriage was falling apart and I couldn't do anything about it because I didn't know what to do. I definitely didn't want to get divorced. All I ever really wanted was to be loved, have a husband and kids and the house with the white picket fence. Because I didn't want to give up on my marriage; I thought all I needed to do was try a little harder. I soon came to find out, it doesn't work when it's a one-way street. I guess you could say I loved him more than he loved me.

Our ideas of love were totally different. I came to realize relationships like marriage don't work if only one person is trying. It takes two. Knowing all this, I still wanted to try to work this out. But I was powerless over his heart, feelings and thoughts.

I had felt like I lost everything and yet the pain wouldn't stop. We shared custody of the girls and by this time, my son's father came back into their life. He was now married and very happy. My soon to be ex-husband had moved on and my life was in great turmoil. It wasn't long before I started selling drugs in the club. I started using the drugs that I sold. It seemed like I became my own best customer. I really tried to get a hold of myself and get a grip but I just couldn't' keep myself together for very long. By the year 2000, my husband and I had officially separated. He went his way and I went my mine. I put everything into a storage and I moved out of the house that we occupied together as a family. It was just too many bad memories. I ended up moving in with the girl that I worked with in the club.

In 2001, I got into another accident. Some guy ran the red light and a city bus hit us. I lived and went home from the scene but my girlfriend wasn't so lucky. She got mangled in the wreck and many surgeries were to be performed in her future. Even though she lived her life was never the same. I look back now again, and that car accident never even phased me. I believe it's because that's one of the events in my life that I blocked out. Way too much stuff was going on in my life at the time. Delayed trauma, is all I can say at this time.

My life was coming and going and all of us girls that worked together (my dancer friends) were all going their own separate ways. One served a fifteen - year prison sentence, one left the country to Hungary, one moved to Oregon and one killed herself. For the first time I was all alone. As I look back now, I was never really alone. *God was always with me. Had I forgotten Him yet again?* I questioned myself.

On this present day as I proofread I realize by looking back over this last paragraph, the presence of God has always been surrounding me and it's because He loves me, plain and simple. ***Hebrews 13:5 (NIV) "Never will I*** *leave you; never will I forsake you."* I had to go back and get my bible, so I could actually see and hold the *Truth* in my hand. Addicts like me always speculate and analyze things and for me I needed to see it, feel it and hold the proof in my hands before I can believe and accept it. And that's how I got to where I am now.

Chapt. 5 – Brokenness

I'll tell you, 2001 was a bad year. That same year my sons went to live with their father and his wife. I continued to share custody with my soon-to-be ex-husband. After all this I had gotten into many unhealthy relationships. One after another, sometimes just for drugs because they had what I wanted yet I still couldn't figure out what I was doing wrong. I would get the same results. It's what they call today, "cookie cutter relationships." I call insanity. I began slowly starting to check out mentally and emotionally. Without realizing it I brought the following year in with another unhealthy relationship followed by being kidnapped by Christmas of 2002. It was a day I'll never forget. The day after Christmas, December 26, 2002.

Now I'm going to tell you what happened. I kept having this dream. There's something really bad going to happen to me because the lifestyle that I was living. I would have this dream over and over again. I would wake up sweating, my heart racing. Somebody in my dream was telling me something bad was going to happen to me if I didn't stop living the life of the streets. Since this was my life now, the nightmares never went away. I started speaking back in the dreams by asking questions. Somehow, I knew it was God and I begged and pleaded with Him in my dreams to tell me when was this going to happen? With all my certainty and acknowledgement and just as plain as day, (like when I was in the hospital when I was hit by the train), that same firm voice told me, *"It's going to be when you forget your weapon."* I knew this was the truth. From that moment on I made sure I never walked out the house without it.

My **weapon** was a very thin skinny screwdriver that you fix radios with. It had an orange handle on the end and it was just short enough to fit in the palm of my hand. Little as it was, it was definitely as sharp as a steak knife and jagged as a small salad fork. Even though I always would walk out of the house with something to protect me, and saying many prayers, yet I still didn't feel safe. I would start overthinking with fear and doubt, *Maybe I interpreted things wrong.* Looking back today I know it was the devil telling me lies. **...When he speaketh a lie, he speaketh of his own: for he is a liar, and the father of it. John 8:44 KJV** Continuing on with what happened...Even having this screwdriver as my **weapon**, I still couldn't get this dream out of my mind. That voice that I came to trust was gentle, calm but firm. From that moment on, I became totally obsessed about never forgetting my **weapon**.

I started hustling in the streets and doing what I had to do to get what I needed. I needed something, anything to get my mind right. At that dark time in my life I was taking methadone, snorting heroin and smoking crack. It's like I needed something to take the pain away so I didn't have to feel anymore. I did this over and over, so many times. The same old routines not to feel anymore. But still when I woke up in the morning, I couldn't deal with life. I would put my head in my hands run my fingers thru and grab my hair and just cry. I had to get up and out to get my fix so that I can think. Looking back now that was a lot of work. I was desperate for help and I just didn't know what to do with myself. It was like I cursed the day I was born.

My boys were at their father's, my girls were at their father's and I was a mess. Hot mess to be exact. I was depressed and I was getting worse by the day. I had to use drugs just to function. Not knowing or understanding what addiction is, I became lost and wretched. I was losing my mind and nobody could relate to me. I did whatever I could do to make money, by all means necessary. By this time, I felt that if I didn't use something, I began to get sick to my stomach and weak. I later learned that this was called being "dope sick."

I thought, *"Why can't I stop using? Why do I have these dreams? Why did my uncle have to do that? Why do men always leave me?"* And I would answer myself, *"Cuz girl, you crazi, nobody love you, nobody cares and you're going insane."* And the sad part about it all was I believed it. I know now today it was Satan, *the enemy of darkness and evil* telling me that hopeless thinking. I played the host to all those lies and ideas. I really did think there was no help for me and that nothing could save me now but a *miracle.* At this moment, feeling so helpless I saw no hope in sight. Thank God for rescuing me today for I can never be more grateful and humble at this very moment in my life.

Please Note: During the writing of this part in the book, it was very hard for me to get through and write about. I cried many tears and had several terrible flashbacks while putting it all on paper. It was like I was reliving this whole incident all over again of the horrible, horrific situation. And the exposure of the pain and emotions that cropped up during this were almost unbearable. With my sister-in-Christ, typist and friend by my side, as we stay God centered, together, we managed to get through this. In the long run it was well worth the freedom and the peace I gained. Looking back now, I kept strong and brave by saying many prayers and seeking God for the courage to keep on going to get this all out. There are times in this segment of this book that I repeated feelings over and over in different ways. This is what my therapist calls doing *trauma writing as I exposed myself to self.*

It was the day after Christmas and I just got done cleaning a customer's house and he paid me with the check for $50. Since I would have the boys with me for Christmas, I wanted to cook them breakfast in the morning. It was too late to cash the check at the local store so out the door I went. Then I remembered, I didn't have my **weapon**. I was like "Oh shoot! I forgot my darn **weapon**." And I went back to the house and I grabbed it. Keeping my mind on my dream, I felt safe because I had my **weapon** on me. *"It won't be tonight,"* I said to myself. So I continued walking to the store, all the while looking for a ride to a 24 hour check cashing store. There I would cash my check and all will be well and I'll go back home to enjoy what was left of Christmas with my sons. Only thing is that I never made it home.

36

No buses were running and I asked a few people could they give me a ride. They weren't complete strangers. I had seen them around. They were from my part of town. However, I wasn't successful in getting a ride with any them. Then I met a girl that I knew on the street that knew somebody else that could give me a ride. I told him I would pay him. He looked 'okay' I guess his demeanor very polite. Such a bright, white, beautiful smile I thought. as I jumped in his car. We proceeded to go to the 24hr check cashing store it was a little-ways across town.

I started noticing that he started taking all the shortcuts. The guy really started giving me the *creeps*. The road he took didn't have street lights. I thought to myself, *this guy is so weird.* But in his car hanging from the rear-view mirror was an ID with his picture on it and the name of where he worked at. So, I knew what his name was. I knew where you worked at and if anything happened to me. *Yea, I would know who did it.* So, I thought, *well it won't be tonight because I got my **weapon** in my pocket.* We went to making small talk and he told me that he had to make a stop. He claimed that he was watching his sister's bird and that he had to feed him. We proceeded to a gated community that had a guard at the guard box equipped with several cameras. I worried about nothing. This stranger had earned my trust.

He asked me to come upstairs if I wanted to make a few more extra dollars. I thought, *Well yes. What's the harm in making a little bit more money?* That was the worst mistake of my life. Not only did he rape me, rob me and beat me when that was over he told me to get dressed cause now it was time to kill me cause I would tell. Also I was to hand over to him my phone, my gold jewelry, the money he gave me and the uncashed check for $50. Just as I handed it all over to him I started shaking as I panicked with fear. I had to make a quick decision.

So I dashed to the front door as he raced with me and beat me to it. Because he got there first, I couldn't open it in time and he caught me. I dived under and wrestled with him underneath the glass table in the dining room; wedged myself between the chairs like a snake. It was then I was able to reach into my front pants pocket for my **weapon**. It was then I felt the handle, grasped it and positioned it for a jabbing motion when the time was right. He dragged me from underneath the glass table and we wrestled all the way back down the hall back into the bedroom. This whole time he was uttering how stupid and dumb I was to ever get in a car with someone like him. He then told me what he was going to do with me so I won't tell.

The whole time I was begging and pleading with him that I would never tell. *"Just let me go home to my kids,"* I said screaming for dear life. Once again, all I had was God to help me get through this. *It* bent my middle finger backwards, as if to break it. But no matter what, I didn't let go of the **weapon** in my hand. *Creepo* didn't like this and he dug his finger in my right eye. Oh, I felt something warm go down my cheek. It was my eye and blood laying on my cheekbone. It brought me back to the memory of the high chair incident again. It was my motivation to stab him with all my might at every opportunity I could get.

Every chance I got an opening, I stuck him again and I stuck him again. I stabbed him and I fought for my life and I thought of my kids. If I didn't know much at this time, I knew for certain that I didn't want to die like this by the hand of a man. I was determined to live. I had kids to take care of and get home to. I had to seek God. I knew the only one that can help me now was Him. I couldn't understand this, I had my *weapon* with me. Why did this happen to me? I listened and for a second and I got mad and I thought *God wasn't on my side.* It was just then my best thinking came into play at my worst time and I realized, *I did forget my weapon; I just went back and got it.* I regained more strength and continued to keep fighting. I continued to hold on. I was determined I was going home to my kids tonight. This guy was not about to take my life. I never wanted to die at the hands of *a weird ass psychopathic man at that.* With the thought of this it only made me want to fight longer, stronger and harder. It was then that he pushed me against the wall and then the window. We were on the second floor of this condo apartment building, and because I wouldn't let go of my *weapon* in my hand, he pushed me one last time with great force. I hit the window behind me with such force that it cracked. We both heard it. It was then I looked into his deep, dark, black eyes, like he had no soul and no conscience. He smiled and I smiled and I knew what his next move was. He pushed me so hard and I felt the window give way. When I went flying out that window, I grabbed him by the scruff of the collar of his shirt and I proceeded with all my might to hold on and took him with me. I thought, *"If I'm going, you coming too,"* with a lot of cuss words in between the thoughts. Lol.

We fell out the window on our backs with the top of our heads touching. As I rose up, I grabbed the piece of glass that was shaped like a machete, and I proceeded to cut his throat. It was only by the grace of God that I heard a women's voice saying, *"Stop! Stop! The police are coming. We heard you screaming. Don't do it! Calm down. They're coming, they're coming! Coming!"* Then I went into shock. I was so mad at God, just for another second. '*Why would God let this happen to me?* Then I remembered again, I had forgotten my *weapon* this night but I went back to get it. God did tell me it would be the night I forgot it. God did block my death and once again my life was spared.

I ended up getting my right eye almost gouged completely out by this psycho's pointer finger; punctured and swollen beyond belief. I looked terrible. I was now a victim of rape, assault and battery, robbery and attempted murder. The police took pictures of the crime scene and charges were placed on the assailant. He turned out to be a very dangerous man that preyed on women. I learned a lot from this incident about myself, God and ones of the opposite sex. Lesson one: ya cant trust nobody in the streets on their looks. God saved my life and I am sure of His voice and I needed serious help for me. My addiction became chronically out of control. Lesson two: **2 Corrinthains11:14 HCSB-**

For Satan disguises himself as an angel of light. This sure was the truth of this verse.

He was put in jail and released on bond. Before the return of his court date, he had already hurt another woman and a man before he was sentenced. **'It'** pleaded guilty and was sentenced to prison time. I ended up going to much needed, overdue therapy and things started making a little sense to me. By this time, 2003 was here and things were turning around for the better but I didn't know that at the time. I suffered from PTSD and serious panic attacks. Not to mention my drug use continued to get *worser* as the days got longer and darker for me. I got into another unhealthy relationship. This was when I got involved with 'Tae.'

To me this really actually starts my story of how I was so lost, broken, empty, battered, bruised and about all the struggles I went through and how it took me so long to get there. From being in so many unhealthy relationships I learned to never tell a man I loved him first. I would wait until he told me. All men would say they loved me but I knew they were really after something else or my motives were never correct. I would base my love from them on what they gave or what they could do for me. An example was how much drugs they could give me any time I would ask for some. My conception on love was warped and twisted as I look back now.

Looking back now I realized there was only one man I needed. How I searched and searched for true love and now relieved my quest is over. Today my desire is to serve God. I love Him because He first loved me. It says so in **1 John 4:19 KJV We loved him because he first loved us**.

Who I am!

Chapt. 6 - And He Said, "He Loved Me."
Part 1

Tae was the sweetest guy I ever met. This is what I learned. "The sweetest man can also be the evilest man." Unfortunately, I learned that the hard way. By Valentine's Day of this New Year, I would suffer a broken tripod fracture of my right cheek bones and my girls would become a witness to a violent attack on my life from a man that swore he loved me. This is actually where my testimony begins of when I began to notice how God's grace and mercy had already began saving me all along before I even met Tae.

Now, Tae had what I wanted. I thought he understood me. *Wow, I thought this is it; I finally found the right man. I'm in love.* But there was only one thing wrong. He was a *basket case,* straight from the depths of hell. He was very abusive and 'cray cray' because of his jealous ways. I couldn't deal with his jealousy because I had already been through that before. So I broke it off with him. Hell, and I was already not right in the head from my past. Later on that evening, in February, just around Valentine's Day, he broke in thru my window by pulling the AC window unit out. It was then he punched me in the face. He hit me so hard that I spun around and landed on a cement terrazzo floor. He did this in front of my two daughters. My daughters told me later on that they thought he had killed me. They were certainly traumatized and the police were called and took pictures. Tae went to jail and then we went to court for this. I thought it was all over with. But the state had already picked up the charges. It was just a matter of time now before the consequences would begin.

I swore under oath that this was not the guy that broke thru my window. Because I didn't press charges, (for my own good safety reasons), they told me I could be charged with child endangerment for letting a dangerous man around my children. Even though months later I felt that enough time had gone by now (and he said he was sorry) and we got back together on good terms. I thought things would change but they didn't. They must have been watching the house because next thing I knew, the state of Florida pressed charges on me with child endangerment and on April 13, 2003. The Department of Children and Family, we call them DCF or I say 'the Calvary' because they come well equipped with their (police officers and special social workers) whole team in place just in case an unexpected problems happen. It's not too keen to go around taking a parents children without much of a warning. The way it happened though I felt they could of did a better job. They basically snatched up my girls while they were walking to the bus stop.

I was greeted with a hard knock on the door, saying I had to be at court in one hour. After being very disgruntled with the situation that just happened. I went to thinking, *of all the nerve these people have*...as I look back now I was so self-centered, blind and lame. I didn't even have the courage to walk away from all of this mess I put myself and my kids in.

When I finally calmed down, I got myself together, went downtown and from that moment on, life became so real. They weren't going to give them back right away because of my relationship I was in. *Okay. Now wait just a darn gon' minute. What are these people talking about? I only got high once in a while and "Tae" said he was sorry for hitting me. Boy was he sick* but I was even sicker for being involved with him. I was also in denial big time about my drug addiction and me thinking I could always change or fix him, hell I couldn't even fix myself. Boy, talk about codependency I learned this is what you call being codependent and I for sure had it bad.

Part 2

By this time, I was so spiritually, emotionally, physically and mentally bankrupt. I felt so crazly insane to boot on top of it all. "What's wrong with me God?" I prayed. Then I thought, maybe it's the drugs and I needed help. Cool, I go to treatment, get off the drugs and everything will go back to normal. I thought, I'll be fixed. I just needed help. Thinking I could do this by myself, although it worked for a while, it didn't get me very far. I relied on my own self for my own understanding. **Trust in the LORD with all your heart and lean not on your own understanding Proverbs 3:5 NIV**. *How many times did I have to keep this in mind? One of the first things I learned, "If I am the problem, how can I go to myself for the solution?" I surely needed to go down the right path this time and that's where the second part of* **Proverbs 3:6 NIV** *came to mind.* **In all your ways submit to him, and he will make your paths straight.** *But at this time I realized a little too late I went down the wrong path.*

A case plan was then designed for me the day I went to court. I had a list of things to do. I had to go to detox, enroll in a 60-day drug treatment program, take random drug tests, a psych evaluation, and take parenting life skills classes. It was the psych evaluation that made me understand what was going on in my mind all these years. The psychiatrist said, "From what you have told me about your childhood, sounds like you have been severely depressed and it had gone untreated." My diagnoses were tripling times three. For me it was no dual diagnosis. So now severe depression. PTSD and drug addiction. All the trauma and violence it all affected me in the worst ways. I had every normalcy of why I should feel the ways I felt. WOW!!! And I thought I was just crazy and unintelligent. Things started to make a little sense to me now. No wonder as a child to a teenager, all the way from New Jersey to Jax Fl through to WV, I used to go to bed dreading tomorrow with tears in my eyes as far as I can think back. I went to sleep like that for so many years. Sometimes when I couldn't sleep, "It's because you haven't cried yet," I told myself. All I wanted to do was just sleep and sleep so I wouldn't have to deal with my feelings. Waking up in the morning was forever a struggle for me. I had to go to school; that was always better than staying at home. In West Virginia when I was in high school I couldn't wait to get back to my bed and sleep. I always wished I could just sleep my life away like the fairy tale *"Rip Van Winkle."* I also thought of another way I could get out of dealing with life by ending mine but I was too scared to. Who would take care of my cats and my kittens if I wasn't here? I know this might sound silly but loving all my kittens and cats, raising and feeding them, gave me hope to endure more until the next day came. They depended on me. I also needed them just as much.

To sum it all up in a nut shell I didn't know how to cope when life showed up. This was how I began to learn of the power of God and how His strength worked through me. It was Him that saved me because I surrendered and let go.

There was a lot of things I had to do for my case plan. I had a full plate and plenty of work to do. After successfully being discharged from treatment, I had to get an approved, legit job and establish a stable place of residency. And the topper for all this, I had to maintain this for 6 months before they would even consider giving me my rights back. The only way I got through this was when they let me visit my girls. Seeing them gave them hope that we would all be united one day it also assured them to know I wasn't giving up on them. No matter what, come hell or high water, I was getting my girls back and eventually I did just that.

Reflecting back, while still in treatment, just before I got released, it was a Sunday, visitor's day. My mom came to see me. I ran up to her like a lil' girl and anxiously said all in one breathe, "Mommy, Mommy! Look what I wrote! I can write! I can write!" She said, "Girl, calm down. I know you can write. Don't you remember all those stories you used to write in school? You always said you wanted to be a reporter one day or a journalist." I looked at her dumbfounded and said, "Oh yea, that's right. I can." I had forgotten who I was for eighteen years. But most of all I guess really surprised myself when I showed my mother what I wrote. It was on how I saw the colors of active addiction and how I see them now that I cleaned up.

July 2003

COLORS OF ADDICTION

Before Rehab - Negative:

Clear- You could see right thru me. I couldn't hide nowhere.
White- like I was pure; but I wasn't, dingy.
Yellow- caution; in a relapse mode; beware
Orange- I'm thinking, contemplating, things are getting ugly real fast.
Green- I didn't keep it green, so there I was.
Red- I'm hot, off to the races.
Purple - I'm a winner; Yes, I feel good. NOT - LOSER
Blue - I became sad and cried and no one heard me.
Brown- shit is gettin' old; I'm gettin' tired; Old shit stinks.
Black- It's dark; I'm sleeping or wishing I was dead; Nothing matters anymore.
Grey- My soul has rose; And I am dead; There is very little hope.
After Rehab - Positive:

Clear - I'm seeing again. I'm starting to realize things.

White- My clothes are coming clean and so is my soul.

Yellow- Stay cautious; remember triggers are everywhere, beware.

Orange- Living free, free from drugs today and things are better; juicy.

Green - Keep it.   Remembering what it's like; Keep it fresh; Don't forget where I came from.

Red- Recover is on; I am poppin'. Hot, on fire.

Purple- I am a winner, royal, outstanding.

Blue- ...no longer makes me sad or cry.

Brown - Like I like my coffee (Lol). Guess what? Not a bad color after all.

Black- Not such a dark world after all, when you're clean.

Grey- I can find beauty on a cloudy day. And today, I am clean and that's a blessing.

Moral: Don't let the colors of life get you down. Hold your head up high and your eyes towards the heavens 'cause life is about change and what you make of it in all giving and living situations.

Here this whole time, I "had been a poet and didn't know it." Well maybe I knew it but I just didn't believe it. Because I didn't believe in me. And now God had exposed to me my gift of writing. It was only by the grace of God. Till this very moment I give Him the all the credit and thank Him for using me as His chosen vessel to share my story. I then realize again no wonder I never understood what Psalm 23:1 meant. It was on a wooden plaque that I won in Sunday School when I was five for reciting the verse John 3:16. **Psalm 23:1 The Lord is my shepherd. I shall not want. KJV** I was so confused. If He is my shepherd, why don't I want Him? Then it registered. "Want" has another meaning. I shall not want for nothing. It took me all these years to figure this out, with the help of my therapist.   Thank God she was a Christian and she understood, reassured and gave me all the hope I needed at that awaking time in my life.

Fast forwarding a bit, the following bible verse that I had to recite: **John 3:16 For God so loved the world, that He gave His only begotten son, that whosoever believes in Him, shall not perish, but have everlasting life.   KJV**. _Of all the things I would remember, who knew this would be the first words I utter after the first two strokes 13 more years later? Where once again I was saved by the grace of God. This verse has become my whole life verse not knowing what lay ahead of me with Joel._

The Way It Was and The Way It Is Now
Part 3

On the night before my departure (that was set on my birthday).God, myself and a few sober friends I made there brought it in with love. In August that summer I was about to be turning thirty-seven God surprised me with one of the most memorable gifts that I would've never thought was possible. He was always known for providing me with the most awesome gifts. So my departure was set on my birthday the best present ever I thought. I couldn't wait to get out and do the things that required me to get my girls home. That evening around midnight

God brought my birthday being able to see the planet Mars. And I thought, *"Freakin' men are from Mars! Are you kidding me? No wonder they act so dumb!"*

Upon being successfully discharged from drug rehab, I still had to follow a case plan. I went to a sober living facility where I attended recovery meetings daily. We were always held accountable there by our house mother. It was there that I learned of "The Lord's Place." It was right down the street from my son's dad's house. Every two weeks, I got to see my daughters on a Wednesday. I would cook them dinner, whatever they wanted to eat. My sons would accompany me, carrying the food, and to see their sisters. We would all pray, sit down and eat. We were once again a family. Even if it just was for a couple of hours. Here I had my own two-bedroom, two bath apartment, provided by this place. Things were only good for a short time.

While still there at "The Lord's Place," I had a lot of time on my hands to reflect on my past. So, I started writing. I was still amazed about my writing abilities that I couldn't even stop. Words would flow thru my brain faster than I could write them. Letters, sounds, colors. I became so excited for more. It was so therapeutic for me. I had to start getting really honest to myself about my drug use. The effects it had on the people around me. I wrote this poem because I actually suffered from Schizophrenia. Although it went away, without the use of drugs, my past still seemed to haunt me. At the time my thoughts seemed so real. It was the drugs that were causing it. I imagined 'snippers in the trees,' thought 'this house is bugged.' You know, all that crazy stuff when we're paranoid, what they call tweaking. In all actuality the reality of all this is fear. Always being afraid of my own shadow or loud noises when I got high; instead of enjoying the feeling I believe now it was the trip I sought. The delusions and illusions put me in faraway places with mental psychosis. By writing out my feelings seems to be the only way I can heal and move on to own my stuff. It was me this happened because I am allergic to drugs. So here's to all ya'll that thought someone was out to get ya."

It Was Only Me

"Living in the cold, cold world, full of life's uncertainties.
Comes a time to separate dreams from realities."

I suffered from drug induced Schizophrenia,
A disorder of the mind.
Where you can't sleep, can't stop,
Can't feel. Don't know what's fake or real.
I would come out of my room,
Looking all around,
Telling everyone, "Shut up. Be quiet."
Turn that T.V. down.

Heard noises from the walls,
Saw faces in the ceiling.
"Someone's gonna get me!"
Such an awful feeling.

Soooo...............

I grabbed the knife,
Running from room to room.
Looking everywhere, looking all around.
Looking, Looking so many times,
Looking out the blinds.

I did this over and over,
Again and again.
Countless number of times,
Damn! Now the police were coming,
But I gotta get high one more time.
Not really knowing, I was really suffering,
From a paranoid state of mind.

So, it's today I have to own my thoughts,
On how I used to be.
See...
...Nobody was there...
....Nobody was coming...
...It was only me.

Netanis H

Well, since I was getting out my feelings, I didn't stop there. It was then I began to write about "Tae," so I could get some closure. My, my, my...How the pen is sharper than the sword. This is the point I got to in that toxic relationship. It was either me or him. One of us had to go. This is dedicated to all the women who have lived through this. Domestic violence, you understand and I understand. Maybe everyone will listen. This was my way of getting back at him, through this poem. After I finished it I got a stamp and envelope and mailed this to his dad's house with courage, newly profound faith and many prayers.

¿ In Love? Love?

"Dreaming of being in love. Often she wondered. What is true love? She pondered and pondered."

He came as bleak as darkness in the mourning,
With quick fast words of hearts Love-Lorning.
For no one knew of the pain he induced,
Yelled at, spit on, tied up, beaten on, so much drama.
So much abuse.
So confused, is this true love?
She thinks. She thought. Fighting fights.
That was all her fault, was all she was taught.
She knew one day, he'd probably take her life and end it,
Always wishing he could stop, wishing he would quit.
Being love was all that ever mattered.
So use to being used, abused, beaten, and battered.
Then the day came, neighbors heard bangs
And screams AGAIN.
And broke down the door.
There lay a bloody, bloody mess,
All over the place, all over the floor.

Some say, 'She loved herself.'
Yes! That's what they said.
Got two shots through the head,
Stabbed, sliced up, all over
As he lay dead
In the bed.
                        Netanis H.

I saw him again shortly after that walking down the sidewalk coming toward me when I looked back up he crossed over and walked on the other side of the street. I knew then, he had gotten his mail. I smirked with the relief of such sweet revenge. I was no longer afraid of him. I realized then that the pen really is sharper than the two-sided sword.

This next poem also pertained to the abusive boyfriend. I saw him again after I got out of rehab in 2003. I know I had to forgive myself for putting up with his nonsense. He told me he was sorry again for everything that transpired with my girls and the state of Florida. I immediately responded that I was to him "I'm 'scrate. It's the girls you owe an apology to." When I talked to my daughters that I had seen "Tae" they told me, "He can keep that apology." Nothing was gonna change the way they felt. And I didn't blame them either. I couldn't forget how he stayed abusing me in one way or another. So, we departed ways and when I saw him for the third time, it was almost like he picked it up where we left off at. And I wasn't taking his verbal abuse. I was done. It just didn't hurt anymore. So that's when I wrote about how I wasn't affected by him anymore. He just didn't faze me. And I wrote him permanently out of my life again.

It Doesn't Hurt Anymore

The pain, the hurt inside, all those intimate talks
All those lies.
For I tried and tried,
To deny. All those tears I cried,
And cried.
So to get over you,
I mourned you like instant death,
As if you perished,
As if you died.
Netanis L.

It's funny how life shows up and comes around and goes around. Karma really is a B. His life was over in July 2015, right before his 35th birthday. He was gunned down in a drive by and shot in the head. Although he remained alive until Christmas 2017, I found out he accepted Christ as his Lord and Savior. In the end, that was all that really mattered to me. I thank God for the gift of forgiveness because I was able to forgive him and be well with my soul long before his demise. You know what they say, in the streets it's "An eye for an eye." Some people say, "You live by the sword and die by it." My belief is when you're riding by your own self will, you will be dealt the consequences of your own actions. And that's life. It was obvious he had his hurts, hang ups, and addictions but in the end he accepted God. It's never too late to yes to Jesus.

Wow!! What A Year, 'Dat 2003"
Part 4

With so much pressure riding on me getting a job, I decided to go back and dance. My girls were living with my ex-husband and my sons with their father and I found myself feeling empty, depressed and lonely again. It wasn't long after that, that I relapsed. I knew what that meant, I had to leave "The Lord's Place. Right before I left, I would walk in a park by an inter-coastal waterway. There was an old boat pier there made out of weathered old wood that was deteriorating. Even though it was blocked off, I would walk around the caution tape and just stand there. I wrote many poems walking by the park, by the inter-coastal waterway; It became my inspiration for one of my books I would be writing titled, _As Told By The Sea Shore,_ as I would later name it. And one of my last days there before I relapsed, I wrote _In A Heartbeat._

I found out that a lot of the people I just went to treatment with had either relapsed or died suddenly. They often told us only one or two of us would make it. I just knew that they were not talking about me. And so it goes like that. People, places and things, and for me, not exactly in that order, but it eventually happened. Here is one of the poems that I have had the pleasure of writing just once. As I walked along this pier, the sun was going down about 8:30 pm in the summer. And as I was walking, I was thinking. _If they only knew what I could see. 'Shoot,' if only I knew that this was just the beginning of my long hard journey._

In A Heartbeat
On an old rugged broken down
Wooden pier I stood.
Lookin' as the sun shined off the oceans wake.
Wondering if I could walk on water like Jesus could.
>   Or… maybe die for sick and suffering addicts
>   Or… maybe my sight, He'd take.
>   As… I closed my eyes,
>   So… I could only hear the birds' voice
Hoping that no more addicts would ever die
Cause my blindness would by my choice -

To stipulate the fact, that I would never
Back down to God's word, Never to retreat.
I would gladly give up my sense and go blind
For the meager, and the weak
>   I would do this:
>   In a second
>   In a moment
>   In a Heartbeat.
>   Netanis H.

Since the New Year had touched down, Christmas of '03 was a great big blur for me. I met an old friend and he offered me a new place to live and a new start. I then packed up my stuff and I moved in with him. His name, "Taximan." He had a daughter the same age as my girls and she wasn't allowed to see her mom. I believe God put us together for that reason. She missed her mom and I missed my daughters. So, we comforted each other so much. God had always seemed to put the right people in my path at the right time.

By this time the state gave custody to my ex and he said that I could see them when I got a stable place. And I did, thanks to "Taximan." Even though they didn't actually live under my roof, I still got to see them every chance I could. In December 2003, me and my husband divorced, bringing in 2004 with a *bang* for the new year. Literally that's how it started to play out and the bang was not from a gunshot (pun intended).

Chapt. 7- The Rest Of The Story Of 2004

Living at "Taximan's" house was challenging at times. Being as the girls were at my ex's house, there was relief but very little at times. It rained so much that spring and summer. And the hurricanes Frances and Jeanne were making their way across Florida's east coast in 2004. However, I had my own hurricane to deal with, "Hurricane Tina." I was a category zero; it was off the map. One of the worse ones to hit Florida since the first one recorded in 1928, before they gave them a name. They were named by the year. So that was the case with me then. 2004. "Hurricane Tina," what a mess I left in my wake, flooding with watery tears. And although my storms were over for a while, they surely followed me in a path of havoc and major destructiveness.

Since it rained so much, I would go outside on the halfway enclosed porch while it was raining and wrote. I felt like a failure and sought God again. For I didn't want to make a mockery out of God's gift he gave me, so I continued to write poems but very little. Who knew I was in such pain? I surely didn't let anyone know that. That was a "no-no." I wrote this next poem at this time in my life.

The Painless Rain

Love the rain,
Takes away the pain.
Not to remember the
Full winter cold December.
Like the tears that flows,
The wetness goes.
The rain doesn't change,
The dew,
Stays the same.
To love the rain,
To take away my pain,
Yet still…
Loving the rain,
Taking the pain.
Winter remembers,
Dark Decembers,
And snows so cold,
Death grows old.
Still it rains. And nothing changed.

By Netanis "Angel Star" Lopez

"I might have lost the battle, but the war is not over. I have not yet begun to fight." – John Paul Jones

John Paul Jones couldn't have said it better. I didn't know the words of that Naval captain would have so much more meaning to me in the years to come. After so many twists and turns thus far, I began to sink slowly in quicksand and there was no one there to throw me a rope. I had lost, I wrote things that were lies. You know like when you can't walk and chew gum at the same time? For instance, I can't write and get high and/or do drugs at the same time. It's one or the other. Since the disease of addiction was back active in my life, running rampant, it only continued to get worse. That year in 2004, "Taximan" was a diabetic so I stole his syringes from his top drawer. From being in rehab, I got the scoop on how to use I.V. league style. And the song, *"Boy, I Wish I Never Met You,"* came to mind. I played with this rollercoaster for a while, named "Speedball." I still managed to work, keep money in my pocket, and straighten up on the weekends to see my girls. But my girls were not stupid. They knew. But they didn't let on, till later.

At this point in my life I had nothing but my writings. That seemed to be the only thing that made me feel better. When I wrote, I could see my reality. And nobody knew that anything was really wrong. It's like I looked good on the outside but on the inside, I was dull and empty. Waking up in the middle of the night, when I could sleep, my mind would race with thoughts and memories of the past. I stayed living in regret. I wrote on a piece of paper and called it my journal entry and the words speak for themselves. My grandmother used to have this steel iron plaque of the Dutch would say when she lived in Pennsylvania. *We grow too soon old and too late smart. - Dutch Proverb.* For some reason this came to mind. I pondered and pondered this thought until I finally got up and started doing what I do, writing. Eventually it came out…everything I was feeling was all on paper, thinking to myself, *with doubts, Will I ever live long enough to write my book? Will I ever learn? Will I ever stop using? Will I ever get this? Why me?*

And who would know the answers to all these questions would be revealed (and then some) during the writing of my book with the exception of the last one, Why me? But before this book would be over by seeking God in prayer I would come to know the answer to that. It was simple, so simple. Why not me? Duh. I told myself, laughing hysterically in the library as the people around me say, "Shhh." If they only knew how thankful, silly and humble I am for the Lord favoring me. For I am a strong warrior, survivor of many battles and an overcomer. I am chosen. I feel like the Lord has handpicked me for the day to come to fight in His army of when Jesus comes back. The proof is looking to how He chose all 12 of His disciples. I was a fisherman, a thief, a tax collector, a pessimist, a drunk, a politician. Let me explain. I fished for men, I took their money, I collected my drug money, I was prejudiced, I drank, then I turned my life around when I met Jesus.

Journal Entry

Now my babies gone to the state,
From abusive "Tae," and getting high,
To escape my fate.
My ex left me behind,
When I said, "Let me be,"
What I meant was "Let me be me."
Now he's missing,
Another lips he's kissing,
And now my heart breaks, my life.
I'll soon take, when I awake.
Tell me am I dreaming? Tears steadily
Streaming down my face, this place.
This space. All messed up inside I cried to myself,
To myself I lied. My life I take tomorrow,
When I die. Or living my life in misery.
Waking up, I made a choice.
I prayed for answers,
And this is what I wrote.

Yesterday's Memories

"I slept away my dreams of tomorrow,
Sorrow crept through my mind as
Sadness filled my heart. All I could do
Was pray and that soon followed."

I slept away my dreams of tomorrow,
Sorrow filled my heart and I watched in horror,
Begging God to stop, make it go away
The harder I prayed on my knees,
Every night every day.
So good but yet no so far,
Must I remember, I'm an angel, a star
Within time, past by, I regained my sanity
    And my mind eased.
Asking God please make the pain go away,
    Finally, it ceased
As I slept away the hurting, aching, painful
    Memories of yesterday.
                    "Angel Star"
And that's how I brought in the year 2005, sleeping right thru it and I just couldn't take it anymore. And when I woke up, I read what I wrote. And wrote some more and wrote No More.

No More

"So the day came when she went leaving all those she loved, all those she adored. Her mind set. She just couldn't take it no more."

The sorrow in her eyes, was-
More than she could bear, more
Than she could stand.
Dying on a rainy, grey and
Cloudy day, which is what she wanted.
Always struggling with her mind,
While her heart ached, and memories of
'It' haunted.
Slowly the earth opened, and finally
Came to a close, as they lowered her
Into the ground.
I remember longing for joy, love and
Happiness that she never found
For they didn't quite understand the
Reasons of 'er easiness,' of her many tears.
How she fought the war, losing the battle,
All those damn years.
Now the time has come, for it is here.
Going to a better place, where this is
Nothing to fear.
Not so certain, but one thing is
For sure, me
That their momma was not in pain,
And she didn't have to hurt, "No More!"

Jane Doe

Jane Doe Definition: an unknown or unidentified female person.
And the Jane Doe is me. Looking back, I didn't know who I was, where I was going and I didn't want to be identified when my death was discovered. My shame and foolish pride kept me hidden in the darkness of my useless life of the guilt of failure.

Up until this point when I wrote this, I sometimes thought of taking myself out again but without another thought I would grab my pen and journal it all down. Sooner or later I would eventually write myself 'out' of that feeling. I would pray then go sleep and sleep soundly. About 3:00 am I would awake with many words swimming around in my head. I'd pinpoint the issue that afflicted me in the first place by being totally honest with myself. This is taken from my journal exactly like this:

The Rain,

The devastating pain.
Looking back,
All my stacks,
Drugs gone; wasted
But I swear I can still taste it-
And my mind wouldn't let go
Just then I knew
What I had to do..........

Since cleverly, I knew that I was too cowardly to *knock myself off.* I had a choice to make and I decided to live. After writing The Rain, the rain literally stopped outside. I knew what I had to do to not feel like this again (only if I never used again that is). I managed to pull myself together the best I could or the best I knew how at this time. It would be many more years to come along with a lot of self-destruction and stubbornness on my behalf. Before I would grasp on to this concept.

Disclaimer: *I did not ever have to feel this way again if I don't pick-up ever again.*

Me: Like what does this mean? I would ponder that question many times from going into the recovery rooms. When I asked they simply said
Them: Raise your hand and speak up that you need a sponsor and that you're a newcomer.
Me: *What!!* (That was just a little too much information)
Me: sorry I even asked. I murmured under my breath.
Them: Just then someone hollered, "Just keep coming back."
Me: Thinking back those people don't know me. They don't know what they even talking about. I can do this without all that dumb stuff.
Me: Only if I knew then what I know now, I could of saved major life and death health issues in the future to come. But I know now that I just wasn't ready. I hadn't reached that point of *desperation*, something that they would always talk about, yet.

"If you don't know yourself, and you don't know the enemy, you will lose your battle every time. If you know yourself, but don't know the enemy you will sometimes win, sometimes lose. But you know yourself and you know the enemy, you will win every battle." ~ Sun Tzu

Chapt. 8 - "But Why Does Everyone Go Against Me?"

Part 1

From what I read about the Chinese general, his strategy and tactics have been known to defeat the enemy. He won more battles than he lost. I believe, even though it doesn't say it in the history books, he believed in a God of his own understanding. As for me and contemplating suicide in my mind I had to defeat my own demons with myself to conquer the haste decision of not taking my own life. If anyone reading this can relate, you don't have to end your life. You can choose a different way. I believe God will never waste the pain that we struggle with in this life. He will turn it around for the good to strengthen us so we can help others.

Just after Christmas, we moved out of "Taximan's" duplex. I bought a car, rented a three-bedroom house and things would get better, since I had my family back together. You know the saying, "When nothing much changes, then nothing much changes." Even though I managed to keep a handle on things on the 'outside,' on the inside behind bathroom doors, things only gotten worse. I could only manage to put a couple of days together without using anything. What I didn't know was that that in the years to come, having one day would be a miracle waiting to happen.

The house I rented was located downtown, just a mere 5 blocks away from my ex and his new girlfriend. I didn't care anymore about him. All I wanted was to be close to my daughters. Everything was going as good as I can expect it. I was in the heart of the downtown area, as people say, "the other side of the tracks," the bad side. Where you don't walk late at night, only if you looking for drugs or money. But I didn't care, I had my sons back in my life and my girls visited anytime they got the chance. Heck, they only lived five streets away from me. I promised my kids we would never be apart again. Only God could keep me from them.

By this time, I thought t things were looking up. I had money, a house and I was back at the clubs. I went back and forth from the Mermaid to the Kitten Klub at all times. Seems like when things start going smoothly for me, someone or something happens that takes my peace of mind and steals my joy.

A few days later my daughters came over, they had these looks of disappointment written all over their faces. Finally, I managed to get it out of them. What had been bothering them? Their father's girlfriend was pregnant. "That girl," is what I'll call her. That's all she was to me. So, in this segment that's how I will be referring to her. (God bless the dead.)

She was a cute girl. Been in the streets at a young age and she couldn't stand me and the feeling was quite mutual. We never got along. We even fought once or twice. But that's how it was. I was powerless over that situation and we moved on. By the end of 2004, Florida had already suffered Hurricane Frances and had hit Palm Beach County and Jeanne right behind her. Moving into the house on 19th Street had its ups and downs.

I applied for a job at the VA Hospital. I got the position at the hospital working in escorting but don't get it twisted, I was supposed to be transporting patients them from one end of the hospital to the other. Needless to say, I never accepted the position because Hurricane Wilma was on its way by the summer of 2005. I believe she was looking for her best friend Betty, and that's when my grandmother had passed away. I was so devastated. She was my rock and my heart were so broken. There were no flights to New Jersey and I wasn't able to attend her funeral. This actually happened to me sometime between Halloween and Thanksgiving. I was still on this earth, but my life on the inside went to the pits of darkness. I know what happened to me but I couldn't put it into words until five years later.

It was like I was stuck somewhere between heaven and hell. Purgatory of my own miserable deadly existence. You know you in bad shape your kids draw sketches of you how you really be looking. And the sketches were never far from the truth. I felt ten times as worse inside.

When I look at this sketch now, I see the pain and the emptiness of my soul. I can't believe I was such a fool. But isn't that what God loves... Babies, fools, and addicts...? Yes, I believe He does. At a time in my life I was all of these and then some. Such foolery and mischief was I. The brokenness of my heart, soul and mind kept me in such bondage. Unknowingly at the time I didn't know how to escape the pain and jaggedness of my sorrowful spirit. I was so afraid of my own being for such a long time. I never thought I'd be afraid of making/having money. Just holding it in my hand and knowing what I was getting ready to do with it made me so fearful and scared. I was so anxious that I would have to use the restroom.

When they say money is the root of all evil, they ain't lying. *For the love of money is the root of all evil...and pierced themselves through with many sorrows. 1 Timothy 6:10 KJV* Today I look at myself and see how far I've come, all the warped thinking I did and all the negative reactions it brought me and I choose not to live that way anymore. Today I don't have much money but I'm full of happiness. The riches of the fruits of the spirits can't be bought. Therefore, I have confessed all my sins and repented. And I know that I am forgiven. Just like it says in the Word: *Repent, then, and turn to God, so that your sins may be wiped out, that times of refreshing may come from the Lord. Acts 3:19 NIV*

The Rest Of The Story
Part 2

October 23, 2005 - My Grandmother
Betty Clein - Sunrise 7-23-1929
        - Sunset 10-15-2005

My Grandmother answered her phone. The caller was Jesus; it was time for her to come home. I dedicate this portion of the last chapter of year 2005 to her.

"Lookin' out my window on a cold and cloudy day,
When I saw this hearst come
A rollin', for ta carry my mother away.
So, I told that undertaker, Undertaker
Please drive slow, for that woman
You're a haulin',
Lord, I hate to see her go...

By June Carter-Cash

June and Johnny Cash had both passed away just a couple of years before my grandmother in 2003. They were my grandmother's favorite singers. She used to say, "That Johnny Cash, now he's my man! Too bad he's married to my friend June Carter-Cash."I like to think they were at the Holy Gates of Heaven to sing to my grandma when she arrived.

Going back to the Mermaid, was trying at times. And the guys would keep coming back. Long after they were broke, it's like they were lured in by our beauty. You know like real mermaids that lure in the sailors off the ships, as if to be in a trance of enduring love. But it was just an illusion, a fantasy; all us girls really wanted was their money. And then we'd send them home broke and alone, assuring them we would see them again next time when they come to town, for that very special dance. I wrote a poem about what I thought where the Mermaids came from since they were not real, for no one has really captured one. My grandmother said that people used to call her a witch cause her family was from Salem, Mass. During this time, when they had the Salem Witch Trials,

59

innocent ladies were burned at the stake. Most of those women were just liked to grow herbs for healing, just like modern day herbalists that grow marijuana for recreational use. In those days, that was enough to get you to say you had some special powers cause town folks did the healing and fevers were broke. If that was today, all my friends and most of my family would've been hung. Lol. Because the CBD oil that's out and the plants that are taken from it heals a lot ailments, pains and aches. So with saying this it's how I believe mermaids came about in my imagination.

The Explanation of The First Mermaid

Death of absence,
No longer they find,
Of morbid riddles,
And fatalities to unwind.

Through panic and terror,
Seek no answers abide
Stuffed up;in trunk locker inside.
What's left but clues,,
To a mystery at flank,
When dropped in dark seas,
From the wooden plank,
Slowly it sank.
Innocence prevail,
Confessions denied.
As town folk listen,
And kin folk cry.

Matters seem factual,
Non-fiction comes truth.
Too soon in passing,
So young in youth.

Patrons mourn a lady,
So beautiful that be gone.
Through years, and decades
They weeped, and weeped,
Became weary
So long…so long.

Answers?... Yet…
Still wait to unfold,
Dumped…deep on the bottom
Like bait is a tale told:

She bore a name to rectify, a witches' stench.
 Upon a noose hangs a bitches' wench.
Under the seas, enchanting,
 sirens sea nympho's sang 'bout,
 When opened the chest,
 Alive she came out.
For a mortal she's no more,
 Breathing in water,
Compared to Earth,
Where breathing is harder.

Distinctly, indefinite, shining,
Blinding Scales,
Long golden pearls in hair,
With - unique, shaped,
 Slimy fishtail.

Once was sacrificed,
As sailors' ships sank,
That come to 'er aid,
An explanation... of the....
... first mermaid!!

With this poem I was able to put closure on my grief for a very brief time. But it was enough to get me through the moment. That void in my life was going to eventually exploit me back into darkness once again. At that moment in my life I didn't know Jesus like I know him now. There is nothing that (when life shows up on its own terms) that you can't get through without Him. NOTHING!!! Which reminds me of the bible verse:

1 Corinthians 10:13
... No temptation taken hold of you but such as is common to man. But God is faithful; He will not suffer you to be tempted beyond that which ye are able to bear...

*This was the beginning of death in my life. "God gives and God takes away." This year was nearly over, something had to give. I believe that when you've done all you can do and you're at your wits end, that's when God usually shows up. And that's exactly what was starting to take place, the joy of a new life to come....****The LORD gave, and the LORD has taken away; blessed be the name of the LORD. Job 1:21 ESV***

But he said to me, "My grace is sufficient for you, for my power is made perfect in weakness." Therefore I will boast all the more gladly about my weaknesses, so that Christ's power may rest on me. 2 Corinthians 12:9

Chapt. 9 - Death Was Here & More Was Near
Part 1

I was full of excitement, a new year, a new arrival, Baby T. She was born on March 15, 2006. She brought much joy to our home. I was happy that first spring. She was beautiful. What an angelic looking bitty, lil' teeny weeny lil' thing she was. She was perfect. I never got the chance to see her till she was two weeks old. It was the day I fell in love with her. It was like I fell in love all over again. She looked exactly like my two daughters when they were that old. I didn't get to spend that much time with my girls when they were that age due to working all the time, going to college, and taking care of my husband. So more or less, it's fair to say I took care of everyone else first and placed myself on the back burner at all costs. Most of the times I placed last place, if I placed at all.

"Dang!! Talk about codependent." I didn't know that word existed until recently attending meetings at Grace Church. And I thought for sure that was me, and I had it bad. But that readers, is another book in itself too, Lol.

Getting back to Baby T. She was my beloved daughter's little sister, for they all had the same father. *"Blood is thicker than water."* That is what they say. Before I knew it I would call over my ex's house asking to watch the baby. I was willing to help out anyway I can. "That girl" and I never saw eye to eye till Baby T came along. We put our differences aside because whether we liked it or not our daughters were sisters, so we might as well to get along. My oldest boy was living with me at the time and also loved his baby sister. After all, the man who raised him was the other father he came to know. Even though he didn't call him Dad, he knew he was his stepdad, and his biological father had married a wonderful Christian woman. To this day, she gets me through the trials of daily living. She saw me at my worse and now she sees me at one of my best. I'm actually fulfilling the dream that I always told her about, writing my book.

Now that Lil' T, she was sure a handful. But I didn't care. All of us took care of her. We had no complaints. Her mother, however, had to deal with her own demons, and I knew what she was going through. I didn't stop using but I stopped using the "IV league way." You know what I mean? I had a baby to look after now and my baby son was 17 and was about to get married in December 16, 2006. Then go straight into the Air Force. We had a lot of planning to do.

I *journaled* often. I wrote very few poems. By this time, I had a lot on my plate and responsibilities. I started to not feel so good. I was getting fevers back to back. What a later learned to be called Cotton Fever. I was turning 40 in August and I had a fever that day. I had to work and a birthday party planned for me later that evening. All my family was there. I made it to the restaurant. My mom, my sister, all my kids and their dates all showed up. I went to work later and made a lot of money in a few hours. It was really sticky at the end of August in the summertime. Things were going good again. Money and friends were plentiful but my journals consisted of pain. I was in so much pain again in my heart. But Lil' Baby T, now she made me feel like I had a purpose.

I told myself, I have another chance at my life. So, I managed to put more time together. I went to meetings, dialed the numbers, instead of filing the numbers. To my dismay before 2006 was over, in December all the plans I made fell into a million pieces.

Uhgg...Life Nevr' Stops..
Part 2

On December 15th, the day before my son's wedding, I was put in the hospital. My oldest boy had called 911 on me. And when the first responders came, they said her skin looked of a plumbeous in color of a tarnished silver spoon. The word they used was *lifeless body.* They had never seen a person turn that color and still be alive. They thought I had food poisoning, or a virus or the flu. I wasn't dope sick; I wasn't thinking on those terms. Because I was too sick to even use. I couldn't even realize I needed medical attention. He had tried to call the paramedics days before but I insisted this would pass soon. Well it didn't. I only got worse. My daughters even urged me to go to the hospital but I refused. I didn't want to miss my son's wedding.

I did miss it though. The reception, Christmas Eve, Christmas Day, my son's going away party to the Air Force, New Year's Eve and New Year's Day. Although they brought the wedding pictures into the hospital, I was so sick to even enjoy them. My son's bride, my mom, and all my kids; I felt like I had disappointed everybody. *'In the darn H'* I thought in regret. And they still didn't know what was wrong with me. I've been in here for over ten days by now. When they finally figured it out, they gave me nuclear meds. After administered the medications, I was put under a machine to find where the infection was coming from and I lit up like a Christmas tree. And all roads lead to my heart. After I have been hospitalized for almost two weeks, I thought sarcastically, *Wow ya think after all the tests...* they finally found what was wrong with me.

I had Endocarditis. It was the result of joining my own interpretation of the street *"IV league."* These were my consequences of the result of using drugs that involved needles. I brought in the New Year 2007 while still in the hospital on a six week stay. What I never realized how bad of a decision I made by joining that *league.* I failed to tell the whole story to the doctors and my kids *of why* I got so infected. It was because I broke a big piece of the needle in my arm. My results (that didn't come for four weeks) were high fevers, extreme fatigue, and extensive hospital stay. That stay (I could never get that time back) cost me quality time with all my children. I lived with that regret for almost ten years. Looking back I realize now I had my first war with Endocarditis. Having that infection was one of the hugest battles I ever had to fight, not knowing at the time that I would catch it a couple more times before I would stop using.

64

On December 19, 2006, my oldest daughter came to see me with one of those looks in her face and I can tell by her eyes something was wrong. It didn't take much for me to get it out of her. With tears in her eyes, I knew something drastic had happened. It was then that she explained to me that their dad's house *had the door kicked in*. Yup the feds came and raided the house, took him to jail and hogtied and handcuffed my girls. My daughter then expressed to me how scared they both were and nasty the cops were. For some reason they thought my oldest daughter was *That girl*. She later came after about four hours of being questioned and interrogated by police. Since they didn't have anything to do with their father's wrong doings, they were released on the spot. Later that same evening my girls were placed in *That girls* custody. Needless to say, my ex was locked up in the county, awaiting trial and a six year federal prison sentence was later induced.

Thank God for *That girl,* her name was Katia. Now she took care of business when it came to taking care of the kids. She made sure they, (even my oldest son), had a nice Christmas and New Year's while my little dumb-self stayed in the hospital trying to get better. Katia would bring the baby to see me and make me feel better and I did. We became close, like sisters, like a mother and daughter; for we both loved the same man and bore babies from the same blood. I knew I had to hurry up and get better and stay well so I can take care of things too and help out the best way I can.

I can say this, I truly loved her and the baby. I still have her picture holding Baby T above my bed, along with Joel's next to my grandmother's. I believe these to be all the angels God has sent to watch over me on this present day. With the confidence I have contained in myself by the Unseen is my guarantee of Gods guiding system; this has successfully directed me correctly today and in my past experiences. But don't just take my word my proof is in the WORD. not see **Hebrews 11:1 NIV- Now faith is confidence in what we hope for and assurance about what we do not see.**

Jeremiah 17:7-But blessed is the one that trust the Lord whose confidence is found in Him.

Chapt. 10 - New Beginnings
Part 1

I was discharged late that evening on a very cold, crisp winter night, January 31, 2007. Finally, I can start fixing what's been broken, but not starting with myself cause the doctors already done that. This marked the beginning of my new year. I could go not go wrong. No more fevers, no more pain. I was drug-free, (except the prescriptions, I was given). I was home now and things would soon be back together or so I thought. My girls, my oldest son, and my new edition to the family Baby T was with me. My baby boy was married. I let my ex-husband's girlfriend move in all the way. We all welcomed the new editions to our blended family. This all was supposed to just be temporary; just until everyone got into the groove of things.

Just when I thought things were right, I got hit smack right in the heart with another one of "life's curveballs." February 11, 2007, woke up early, got Baby T from her resting place and put her into the car for a ride. We went for a ride on the inter-coastal and waterway. She was acting really cranky. I was wondering why she was acting this way, usually a ride would calm her down. Just then my cell phone rang. It's one of those calls you only fear about, wishing you would never get. I would never forget that call. There on the other end was a man's voice I didn't recognize, nor this number. A man's voice said, *"Dis Tina, Ahh. Look auh ya gir, aah there's somtn' rong wit 'er. I can't wak 'er up."* He asked me so many questions so fast, I didn't have time to think. Frantically I replied, *"Wat u kall'n me for? Kall 911. Then call me back. Cuz I don't know where u live."* I glanced in the back in the car seat at Baby T and my heart sank. I was saying to myself, *"Oh My God, No, No, No."* With tears filling my eyes, I could barely see but I made it back to the house. I proceeded to call someone to help me get there. Then I realized I didn't know where "there" was. Before I could think to call this unknown number back, the cell phone rang again. This time it was the sheriff's office asking do I know such and such. Then the deputy said, "You need to come to this address and identify her body."

I don't know how I made it to the house in one piece. I had gotten a hold of a friend and the rest is shaky. I know then that God was carrying me thru all this. So I got a grip on myself. I got her stuff the police gave me and my ex's truck that she drove to this guy's house. I grabbed her phone, keys, and the clothes she was wearing. I was once again lost; this was all too much. But I thought of the last 10 days after I had gotten home and all the events that had led up to this moment in time. Little did I know it would only get a lot worse before it got better for many more months to come.

Flabbergasted, As I Gasped For Air
Part 2

Backing up, going back to the night I returned home from the hospital, after being there for six weeks, I found out that our house has been robbed, our screen T.V. gone, son's PS4, CD's included, games, and movies. My son's so-called friend did this. My son dealt with this boy at a later date and situation got handled *ghetto style*.

Flashing back when I walked in the door, the evening of the 31st, the baby came to me with arms wide open and she hugged me tightly and gave me one of her big sloppy kisses. And I hugged her back dearly. Her mother was stepping out for the evening and that was that. We didn't see her for a few days. She returned to bring diapers and food, etc. to see Baby T. See, she loved her mama and she cried for her a lot. This night was no different. And I would always comfort her the best I could to just love on her.

That night on February 10, 2007, I had gotten a phone call from Baby T's mom. And she was checking on her baby like she always did. When she was finished, she would always talk to my daughters and then finally me. She expressed how much she cared for us and told all of us that she loved us. When I got on the phone, she told me to take care of her baby because the day before we had papers drawn up from a notary at the funeral parlor to "make it official." Temporary custody for legal guardianship so I could take care of Baby T. Come to find out that Katia was facing four years' prison time and I agreed. Baby T was already a part of our family so we did it legally. I should have known then something was up.

The dark days were upon me now. Just when I thought things will get better, they didn't and I would see more pitch-black days ahead that I couldn't put a name on the "color" of it. *"What comes after blackness?"* Hmm. *"Death."* I thought and wondered.

We had her funeral in February, which just happened to be my ex-husband's birthday. Although he couldn't attend the funeral because the jail and the county said, "No, not their problem and it's their policy." However, his brothers and sister came in from Belle Glade in his place. One of the hardest things I had ever had to do besides telling my youngest daughter "No," is going to Macy's to buy Lil' T a yellow dress to wear at her own mother's funeral. I had bought a silk yellow dress, with shoes to match, way before I had ever got sick from Tommy Bahama's which I only wore once before this. So, I figured I was her mom now, we should at least match colors. Although I had felt like I had lost my best friend inside. On the outside, I kept up my composure. 'Cause I have daughters and a baby girl that is depending on me, so I really had to woman up. I put on my big girl panties and proceeded with caution of the reality of it all by accepting the facts of life and death. For this was how it was going to be. A severe case of *Que Sera, Sera*. Whatever will be will be. And like my mom always used to say, "Honey, death is a part of life." With that I went into "putting on the mask." I couldn't let others see me falling apart. On the outside I looked good and kept it moving but, on the inside, I remained a wreck.

Love Is Love
Part 3

It is the innocent ones that are affected by our actions, so I know I had to maintain and keep it moving. And that's exactly what I did. I took care of her and the rest of my kids but I couldn't let go of losing Katia like that.   Accidental overdose was the prognosis. She was the first addict that I had knew personally that died from a drug addiction. *"Wow, I thought this disease is real."* Well folks, that's not all. Jails, institutions, and death. Oh my. "Well two out of three ain't bad," I said out loud to myself. I have been through both and I didn't die, someone else did. *"Why me? Why did the sheriff office call me?"* I would panic with these thoughts over and over again. *"Are I not my sister's keeper?"* I was angry with God. I would let it go and let God then the next minute take it back. Not realizing that I had a touch of what is known as *survivor's guilt.*

What I came to learn it was a mental condition that occurs when you blame yourself for surviving a fatal incident when others died. In a nut shell I was grieving in my own way by blaming her death on me. Not knowing at the time there was nothing I could of done. I was powerless over her fatal decisions that she made on that unforgettable night when she lost her life. Not knowing what was to come in the upcoming future that guilt, grief and blame would crop up tenfold in the next few months to come. And that's how the next couple months played out. I thought to myself, I can't keep contemplating over and over. So I stuffed it inside many times and prioritized my responsibilities, for I had *"Bigger fish to fry."*

Little Baby T's birthday was coming up. She was going to be one years old. We had some planning to do.   I was kept very busy with the help of one of our neighbors that kept an eye on me, Miss D. I would cry on her shoulders many times and she would always find the words to get me back in focus. For Miss D, I will always be grateful.   She would tell me Honey God don't make mistakes. That was when I read **Ephesians 1:11. God "works all things according to the counsel of His will"** So before I went to bed I read the first chapter of Ephesians and I was able to sleep a little better than the night before. I knew I had to write something about Katia and come to a peace of mind within myself. So I did what I always did to get my mind out of a funk. I grabbed my sword and my shield and wrote *Death Of An Addict.l*

Death Of An Addict I

To identify her body
It wasn't hard to figure
So many times she O.D.'d
Looking like a top model

She left this world on a cool Sunday morning.
Not sure she even died.
How could she pass on?
She said she'd never die that way,
She'd even made a promise.
Sayin' her last words to us –
"I love ya'll" and her baby she'd miss.
Please give her a kiss.
She left this world at a young age,
And a baby that loved her dearly.
Not knowing she was dead,
not known' what she was really feeln'.

"Death of an addict no one can describe.
A sad feeling when someone close died.
They thought they'd changed,
And then they lied."

I *journaled* only when I would go to work between 'dancing sets.' I practically never left home without my 'shield and sword,' (pen and paper). While in the hospital with my first bout of Endocarditis, my oldest son bought me a leather binding journal book that I kept only for my precious baby. How much joy she brought into my life. She saved me from going over the edge many times. I truly loved her. One of my entries:

3-22-07

Tomorrow is Lil' T's B-day. I feel sad
her birth mom can't be around to celebrate
her. She had such a hard life. My heart
still goes out to her. My Ex will never be
the same either.
Why do I do for him, He told
me he appreciated all I've done for him.
Welp. They're calling my name. I gotta
get on stage, my set, don't want to get fined.

3-23-07
12:27 a.m.

1 years old,
'Baby T'
'T' today you played with my hair until

I awakened. Then you smiled beautifully,
And cute. With 3 teeth on the bottom and
2 on the top, your grin is priceless.
Today you were more pretty than
Yesterday. I wonder what new stunt you
Will do today.
Sometimes you amaze me with Joy. You
Make me laugh until I cry with tears of
Happiness. I love you so much. Oh how you
Have changed my life. I want to tell u.
How: Before you were even thought of
I was a bad girl.
And therefore my life
And the way I lived
It followed me until I
Met you. The first
Time I laid eyes on
You, I never forget
You looked adorable.
Like both of your sisters,
Did when they were born.
Your face was round and
You were sleeping, your mom
Had just gotten done breast
Feeding with you.

3-23-07

And now today your
first b-day. Wow, you've
growed. Once again you awoke
up smiling, laying your head
on my shoulder, but I know
you're still sleepy. I got up
and fixed your cereal and milk
and put it in a bottle. You
love it. We went back to sleep
until 11:30, me, u, and cat.
For he's a baby 2. This afternoon
we goin to c dadi.

And we are back. That
was easy. I liked visiting
him. You fell and hit your
head and was cranky too.
Dadi He didn't get a
chance to see your silly
self, all your clown faces.
You make, all the
rubish you speak like a little
bit-e babe. And finally you
gave me a kiss before I

71

went to work. I like your
hugs and kisses when I
leave to go somewhere and
when I return you greet
me at the door, wanting me
to pick you up. And I do.
Then you give me a kiss and
hug my neck and I don't even
have to ask. You have grown
to have your own personality.
You've started me
to pick up a pen again,
to write about you, to
start my writings, and poems
again.

When I went home that night, I stopped at Walmart and bought her an outfit and baby toys for a one-year-old. Who knew that this would be her first birthday and her last? Until this present day, on this day of 2017, March 17th, I am finally writing my book and my journal writings to share with all, my innermost personal feelings and thoughts. Like who knew, that if you told me in 2007, in ten years I would be writing about her, sitting at the dining room table in my oldest son's house in Fort Myers. I converted one end as a makeshift desk, which by the way, I am going to make room for one in my bedroom, by the window that overlooks the lake, and tree just outside my window.

Getting back to the story, I remember the day of her birthday all too well. We went to the pet store and bought a beautiful Betta Fish, with wings, (fins) like an angel. She pointed, I paid. Now this little girl had a kitten, a fish and claimed my Quaker Parrot, Maxwell. We also had a dog Markie, my son bought for protection when 'those boys' broke into the house. Now Markie loved the baby. He would lick her on her forehead. Somehow Markie knew that this was appropriate and she responded by chasing him or pulling his ears, and he let her. But don't let someone else come in the house and go straight for the baby to pick her up. One quick sudden move and he would jump up between them and the baby, with a look of, *'Don't make a sudden move. I don't play that,'* look on his face. The baby belonged to everybody in that house. Yes, she was my baby and I loved her as if she came out of my womb. God had no doubt sent us a baby angel. We all treated her with unconditional love that could only come from God above.

In the couple months that followed, although I picked up my pen and paper again, I basically only *journaled* (and very little), for I was kept pretty busy. There were baby shots to be given, doctor appointments, diapers, and toilet training. All of us joined in on the responsibility of the baby. I was getting a little worn out.

It's not even funny when your kids draw pictures of what you look like before you go to work, make bets on how you gonna look when you come home from work and how you think you look while at work. Sometimes we swear *we*

72

be looking good. And *we be* looking so rough and that's not cute. I would look like this when I left for work:

However, life showed up for me quite often. I did the best I could at the time. Work and the pressure of making money took a toll on me. It seemed like there was never enough (money, time or drugs) and the problems were unending. I had my problems, my kids' problems, and life's problem's on an everyday basis. I did quite the balancing act with my unbalanced self. I would start out looking what I thought was alright. Dancing non-stop throughout the whole night making monies, meeting new guys to make a new customer and partying with chemical substances however I saw fit. Because I was one of the top money makers I always felt like I was the prettiest girl there too. But who really was I fooling? My own self, and I believed and convinced me. Only if others could really know how ugly and useless my spiritual, mental and emotional inner being really felt.

I thanked God (believe it or not) for others not being able to see thru me. What I didn't know was that my negative actions and sneaky behavioral patterns were very transparent. It was just nobody really cared enough to call me out on my stuff and/or they was just as messed up as me or worse. In hindsight all of us girls that were in that adult entertainment business were women who were sexually abused or worse; dancing so we could provide a better life for our family the best way we knew how at that time in our life. Because no one, I feel knew about getting help back in the early 2000's or being honest with themselves, about their past and what really got them into the 'adult biz besides the money. I believe drugs made it easier to cope with life, the customers, our past relationships and the messes we made along the way, especially when you fix yourself up. But I ended up and looked like this when I came home:

Looking at these pictures my kids drew, I was a hot mess. I looked terrible. How could I think I looked so good? I couldn't see the truth because I couldn't accept it.

Just when things were looking better, I was staying clean, going to meetings, and working at the club full time, as I always did from 7:00 pm - 2:00 am. I was used to it by now. With spring on us, the weather was getting hot and sticky. Easter came and went. Summer was around the corner and I didn't even see it coming. I wish I could say we all lived and loved happily ever after, but I would be writing lies. Just when I thought I had another good grip on myself, my home, my health, my life took another turn. The grim reaper showed up again. And once again, I was hit with another curveball. I got the 'bejesused,' knocked out of me, right dead smack from my heart!!

It was a sultry hot day in May when Baby T was called home. I guess her mother didn't want to be without her. She wanted to wait for her baby so they both could pass thru the Holy Gates together. May 19, 2007, a day in my book that will go down in my history of 'Webe G Angels,' for she is the first "Angel Baby," but little did I know she would not be the last.

I Can't Believe This Is Happening
Part 4

I remember clearly, it was a Wednesday. I remember as if it happened today. I was off that day but I went in anyway and called the kids like I usually do. Everything was fine and I told them I would be home around midnight. I stopped at Walmart like I usually did for groceries and made my way home. I got home and the girls were on the porch waiting for me. They helped me put the groceries in and continued to put them away. I checked on my baby like I always do, and I saw her cuddled up, sleeping. The TV was on, and her cat Herman laid at her feet. We went to bed and I went to move her over and she was warm and limp with purple lips. I screamed for them to call 911. The dispatcher instructed my son and I to do infant CPR. Since, I had been trained, I already knew what to do. I thought she was choking, so I proceeded to clear her airway, while my son encouraged me, while on the phone with the dispatcher. My daughters screamed loudly and panicked.

While waiting for the ambulance to arrive, I could hear them. They were just around the corner with their sirens. They took over with the baby. I comforted my girls and told them it would be *alright* as we huddled up in a circle and shouted out the *Lord's Prayer*. I then jumped in the ambulance and drove swiftly to the hospital where she was born at just a little over a year ago. The doctors then when we arrived at the hospital took over and worked on her for over two hours. I was told to go into the other room. It all happened so fast and I was a nervous, shaky wreck.

Everything was closing in around me and nothing seemed to make sense. *"WTH is going on?!"* I exclaimed to myself. The police came and the detectives and I couldn't understand what just happened. They came and told me she was gone. They did all they could do. I was devastated; I couldn't feel my legs. It seemed like hours passed by and I was a mess. When the doctors came back into the room, they said I could go in and see her. I leaned down off the bed and kissed her gently on her soft cool cheek. I said my goodbye to her, mumbling to myself under my breath. I stepped back, walked away and I heard them pronounce her dead.

I didn't know if I was coming or going. I knew Jesus carried me thru it all because I couldn't feel my feet. I was being carried. *"Why?"* I asked myself. *"Was I not worthy of?"* I was numb. Her funeral in the same funeral home in the same room, just months apart. My ex-husband in the county was on his way to federal prison. "Nope," they couldn't let him go to his own baby's funeral. "Policy," they said. I went almost out of my mind. I was so lost and severely broken. At the funeral parlor what stuck out in my mind was the song that Aunt Freda sang. It was the words that meant the most. *I didn't bring you this far to leave you now.*

Not realizing at that time the lyrics were based on a Bible verse in **Philippians 1:6 GNT And so I am sure that God, who began this good work in you, will carry it on until it is finished on the Day of Christ Jesus.** The way I understand this was just like the words in the song; He wasn't done with me yet and He's not going to leave me now in the midst of my grief. I didn't know in the years to come how much this verse would mean to me.

I had to get out of that house. Yes, move, I must move. *"It was that bad ass luck house with too much negative energy,* "I kept telling myself. I know today that I believe there's no such thing as luck as far as I am concerned. It was just life showing up as life does.

Around November 2007, we moved out of that house and away from the downtown area, a different community. I moved with my girls, my son and his girlfriend. At that time, we put everything into storage and moved with a friend 'Charlie,' of course not his real name. But I could call him worse names than that. Needless to say, our stay at his house didn't last long. We moved out just as fast as we moved in. That's how our new year started at the beginning of 2008. We moved to an efficiency right by the beach. So, I went back to work at the Mermaid making that quick cash since the place we lived at the rent was due weekly. By the New Year coming everyone would all be going in different directions.

At this point in my life I was so tired of moving and moving and moving. I would often think about Heaven and how God has a home waiting for me and my kids. I always promised them one day I'm going to buy a house and we will never have to move again. I just kept remembering this verse in the Bible about my Father's house. ***John 14:2 -4 .NIV My father's house has many rooms; if that were not so, would I have told you that I am going there to prepare a place for you? 3 And if I go and prepare a place for you, I will come back and take you to be with me that you also may be where I am 4 You know the way to the place where I am going."*** Today I truly believe in His promises that one day I will go to His house, for He speaks the *TRUTH.*

By the faith I have in this present day that I have become to believe that I found a way.***Because narrow is the gate and difficult is the way which leads to life, and there are few who find it. Matthew 7:14 NKJV*** To simplify what this means to me, out of all the struggles that I've been through I had to learn to trust God, myself and through every lesson there's a blessing in disguise waiting for me.

Chapt. 11 - Life Was Here But I Wasn't
Part 1

My son moved to Fort Myers and found a new girlfriend. My oldest daughter went to Homestead Job Corp. It was the best decision she could have ever made. It was just my lil' girl and myself left alone in this tough world. My oldest girl came home on the weekends and we made it work as best we could. I went to grief counseling; it helped a little. Soon it would be a year since our baby passed away. All I wanted to do was a celebration for her. So, I bought balloons and wrote this poem for her:

Celebration of Death:
Balloons For Baby

"Once there was a baby
whose love you couldn't count
So precious as a
        hummingbird,
So dainty, and
        colorful as a wild orchid"

My love for her
        I could not measure.
For God sent me
        An angel,
        A sacred treasure,
To wipe away
        Lost, hope and guilt.
To do with her
        like my own
            As I wilt.
Gone as a sudden
        as a breeze
            Blown swiftly.
Gone before her
        Time, too soon
Gone before the
        midnight moon.
Her face, her gums
        Her saliva, I miss.
Her walk, her baby talk
        Her sloppy kiss.
To represent herself
        Her bright colors,
The sunshine at noon
To let go, at the
        Beach, each
        One in many colorful balloons.
A celebration of her death -

Balloons, I sent to heaven
Sent many, many
      Eleven and seven
Colors divine against
      The clear blue sky,
Could see them so far
      So far away, so high.
Carrying a message
      To an angel of love
      And so deeply we miss
Saying the "Lord's Prayer,"
      On the waves; sealing
      With hugs, pennies and a kiss.
That day I felt better
      As the sorrow; cut; my heart-
        -sliced,
      That beautiful day at the
        Beach, we celebrated
        Her life.

By N. Lopez

I didn't really write much after this. I just wrote my prayers out. And I relapsed again. I just couldn't take the pain and this was nothing new, because it was all I knew so that I could not feel. I felt that I betrayed God, again. So since I couldn't see Him it seemed to feel better when I wrote to Him. I needed to see my feelings in black and white so that I had proof that what I was feeling was real. And that was my guilt that I couldn't save her, I thought it should of been me. I felt like God was punishing me for not keeping my word to Him. Little did I know at the time that God is not a punishing God. I had taken my will back and that was the consequences for my actions. For I had my own self to blame. Sometimes life can seem so much easier to blame others for things we do, but that was my crap.

Dear God,
8-16-08
    I hope that you're not too disappointed in me. I'm truly sorry for disobeying you. In my heart I'm hurting for hurting you. God can you give me a chance? Just one more time to do the right thing. Please and thank you for my kids. And shelter. And for "Jon," somewhat. Lord Heavenly Father, I stand accountable for my sins today. Please help me to make money, if it is meant. Bless me in the name, of the Father and the Son, and Holy Spirit. I love you, myself, and my family, and kids, and friends. Amen.

Dear God, my Heavenly Father,   *8-18-08*

    I love you. Thank you for my birthday to be 41. Thank you for being able to write, help me carry the message through my writings and let the angels whisper in my ears. Amen.

Jails & Institutions
Part 2

That was my closure that I needed. Our lives were changed more than ever after our baby passed away. My lil' girl and I sent those balloons. We didn't stay in that efficiency too much longer. After that by Christmas time we were on our way to better places. I stilled suffered from deep depression, and I was lost pretty much of the time. It was like I was in a fog and the mist was getting thicker. So, I did what I always did, you know the 'Geographical move.' It was then the thought occurred to me, like they said, "No matter where you go, there you are." That rang so true. So, by the end of the year 2008, we were on the move again. We stayed with another friend of mine. He had an extra room, he charged no rent, but you already know nothing in life is free. You pay some kind of way, so I would house clean for him. We stayed there for Christmas and had Christmas there. By the year 2009 I wasn't exactly where I wanted to be but I certainly wasn't where I was. Shortly after the New Year, my baby boy will be getting out of the Air Force and my oldest daughter would be finishing up at the Job Corp. Things would be better, or so I thought. I started back not really taking life so seriously. Always thinking, It was all my fault. Nothing seemed to help but using. I couldn't handle life without the use of drugs. My heart was so torn and broken apart. I was hurting so bad on the inside. It wasn't long before even the club I danced at (since I was nineteen) would not consider even hiring me back again! Yup, I became unemployable and it wasn't long before I was pulled over for unpaid tickets and went to jail. I tried to run from the police and they caught up with me. I threw in the 'Crazy Card,' and ended up in jail, still! 'Damn,' I mumbled under my breath. On the psych floor, Baker Act is what they call it. Well I thought well at least I can get something for my head. They didn't give me nothing. 'Not a friggin' pill or Tylenol. Zip! Nada. Zilch. Nothing at all. And I was heated, mad, disappointed at myself. I let my own self get to this point. And once again, I had no one to blame but myself. Those damn poor life's choices I made and now I'm paying the consequences for them. Little did I know at this time, this was just the beginning of them. Its like once again I checked out again. When I would begin to come around again I realized I missed the Clinton and Bush presidency and Obama had now taken office.

Once again, looking back God continued to be my strength of how I always managed to hold on. When push came to shove. I believe within myself 'ya really can't break a women or man for that fact that gets their strength from God'. Only my Lord knew of the many more troubles to come that lay just ahead of me. I began to get in more disorderly conducts with the law, my family and more trying times to come. The Lord became my refuge and my safety net to whom I could always run to in times of trials. This even holds true till this day.

Psalms 9:9 The lord is a stronghold in times of trouble

Chapt. 12 – Falling Apart
Part 1

    I went to court and I was sentenced for ten days. I was dope sick and I did my best to stick it out. It was the longest ten days of my life. When I eventually I was released in handcuffs, by the Baker Act, I was hand delivered by Sheriff to the mental illness institution, where I continued to stay for the next two weeks. I contacted my family since my son was home from the Air Force. His father and his other mom came to see me. When they came to visit me, my baby boy bought me a journal and I couldn't wait to write in it about my experiences that had previously happened to me. So I journaled:

April 29, 2009

    Now they just left, this place is a trip. There is people all over the place complaining - clicking-they're all tripping, it's a freakin' nut house.' It's weird, I'm comfortable. All I have is today to be clean and it's better than yesterday. "Amazing Grace," just are my parting words & song.

    Dang the staff here are so mean to these people, and that sets them 'off.' "How can I make a difference today?" "What do I want to share?" "Why?"

    I told my son the truth, and I know I hurt him but they asked and I told. I'm gonna write some new stuff whenever I get the "OK" from the "Doctor."

April 30, 2009

Empty looks on their faces
And how dey paces and paces
So sad that he has forgotten
Stuck in a mental ward
By family and forgotten
I woke up - in a paper gown
On cold steel -
Damn. What I dun-done?
Not a dream - the chills are real.
I wanted to go home - leave
I felt worthless - hopeless
I just wanted the pain to stop.
And wanted and waited and wished I was dead.
Why has God spared me I wondered?

And I think back to two weeks ago,
It was a Saturday like others,
It came like it was supposed to
As I awaken that morning to do 'My Thing,'
Two years straight run,
Such a quick downward spiral.

"Screaming voices -
All around.
Banging - clanging - it's too much -
Too many sounds."
Lost faces - forgotten dreams
Shuffling along - or so it seems.
Much escape the torturing mind-
And find myself -
Just one more time.

On the edge of the bed she
Fakely cried - cried-
Seeking attention -
Cause she could not hide.
Running from room to room -
As others chant- babbling on.
Once so normal - someone done-
Done - them wrong
Forgotten souls - of God's finest made-
Slapped in the face - for money trade.
Who will come get me?

May 10, 2009

Where do I go?
"Go sit down - Now!"
Staff say,
"Child - I don't know."
"But I need to talk"-

"I need a shower"
'Hold on' - wait a minute-
'A sec.' - and
It's been
An hour.

Complaining - "I hate this job!"
"I hate these people"
'Go'- 'get' - 'shoo'-
Gett'n on my nerves -
That's staff for you.

'Wow!' Relations in a mental health facility -
As they sit - in their own mess -
On their own self - maid trip.

Well to make a long story short, I'll tell you what I didn't do. I didn't stay clean like I promised my family I would. There was just too much to bear, too much to handle. I lost my stuff in storage again. I had new charges again. I lost myself again. And this jail thing wasn't over yet.

Later that same year I had a warrant for my arrest for not going to court and not completing a program. I didn't work in the clubs no more because I was completely banned from all of them. I had become unemployable. Nobody would hire me. The word got out so fast of how I went so downhill and the reasons why. I destroyed my car, my trust broken with a guy who had run a successful car dealership. My last *Sugardaddy*. It was more than that, he was my friend. But I was not his anymore; I had ruined the friendship.

I later return home to the house I was cleaning, Jack's house. Only to return back to jail in October in 2009. I knew of the warrant, there was no way I was going to detox in jail again. Before I turn myself in, I was going to admit myself in detox. So I voluntarily waited on a bed and put myself into detox. When I got out, I committed myself to another mental facility and I pulled the 'Suicide Card.' And I told them I was depressed and wanted to hurt myself. When I look back in reality it was the truth. The day I was discharged and clean, Sheriff Probation Officers combed the neighborhood. It was roundup time. I turned myself in, clean and sober, and went before the judge. Because I volunteered myself, took the paperwork with me, the judge took the time off my VOP.

I was sentenced into 45 days. I served 28 of those days in the stockade. The stockade did me some good. I wrote, I had time to get myself together, get my thoughts together. I even met a girl I used to dance with. She had changed too. Things were strict here. I wrote the same poems over again that I could remember. When you're in jail, you'll do anything to pass the time. I guess you could say I accepted my fate. I had a case alright. *A case of "Sera, Sera."* *"Whatever will be, will be."*

I wrote about one inmate that nobody talked to, including myself. She was very unapproachable. What I didn't know was that she just got off suicide watch. Later I heard she killed herself. Nobody knows what others are going through or been through. Today I am careful not to judge others. So I wrote this about the inmate:

Only She Knew

"I saw the pain in her eyes
I felt her hurt
Talk'n to herself-
No mask, no disguise"

I wanted so much to say it's okay
To give her a hug
And to tell her to pray.

But as the night rolled on
So did her pain-
And the way she was feelin'
Didn't know by morning-
A site they'd be seeing.

She took her own life-
A matter of time.
Wishing I could go back-
Talk to her- And change her mind.
But that's not the case-
And now it's too late.
Tragically she died - by her hands -
Her fate.

So the next time
I see those eyes-
And feel someone's pain
I'll shake her hand-
Give her a hug -
And ask her -
Her name.

By Netanis Lopez

Falling To Pieces
Part 2

I was so lost and I didn't want to believe that I'd gotten worse. I was a crazy drug addict now and hopelessly lost. I had this void in my soul of regrets of days gone by. There was no hope for me I thought, 'my life is doomed.' The only thing I knew and had left was my writing out my poems and how I saw life at the time. That was my therapeutic gift of releasing my pain. So that's how I came to write *Hole In My Soul*.

Hole In My Soul

I had a hole
In my soul
And I couldn't figure why?
Remembering so many days
How I wished
I would die
But not today - cause I became
At peace within myself -
-take care of my health
-along comes my wealth.
And life feels good - because I'm
Understood - within me.
Cause I know why God
Put me in here -
And what he wants
Me to be.
And its because he cares.

There is not much to add to this time in my life. Only very few poems and a lot of prayers. These prayers are what got me through the tough times ahead at the stockade. I couldn't believe that I ended up in a prison dorm of the county jail. I was exactly where I needed to be. It's what my life had boiled down to. Sitting here in the drug dorm came to be a reality of my future. And I didn't like it very much. They were so bossy here. You had to make your bed a certain way, three minutes to shower, and up before sunrise. Needless to say I was transferred out the next day. This was not for me. I was not going to comply with those kinds of demands. Plus my stay was just for a little over a month and that wasn't long enough to qualify for the program. What a blessing for me, I thought. I was still able to get information to get help for my addiction though for when I was released. But I cleaned up before I got here and *I would be fine* I told myself. One in particular prayer that I wrote down really sticks out to me today and I

85

wanted to share it with you. It always brings me back to the moment of clarity of how I was so afraid and today I'm not.

7-13-09

I'm Afraid

I'm afraid that I don't
Have another chance
To be what I want

I'm afraid that I didn't
Tell my kids that I loved them enuff.
And that they still don't believe me.

I'm afraid of not going
To Heaven and/or Hell either
And waking up in the middle

I'm afraid that a sunny day,
won't make me tan.

And I'm afraid that I wont
Acknowledge another cloudy
Rainy day, which I love

For these things: I'm afraid of living,
And still not getting to see these things,
I'm afraid.

And then God spoke "My child be not afraid, Be unafraid for I am with you. To guide you every step of the way, even though you don't see me, hold my hand and I will lead you, but you must be first unafraid before we can ever begin." Amen.

This was my take on Imagining what God would say to me. I just felt these words. I guess I was sorta speaking to myself and encouraging myself in the Lord. In *Deuteronomy 31:8 "... Do not be afraid; do not be discouraged."*

Chapt. 13 - Another Case
Part 1

Let me tell you about the stockade. It's for inmates doing more than 10 days. By this time, I've been to jail twice this year. So, I wrote like I usually do. I really didn't know what to expect. Things seemed to be different everytime I would go back to the county. You never know who you gonna see or whats going to happen next.

Monday,
November 3, 2009
I was supposed to figure out what was bothering me. And I think I'm just cold and tired and the medication they had me on is affecting me. And although I know that it can't hurt me, I believe the side effects are harmful. Tomorrow I will go outside, tonight I shall take a shower and I will be okay. It's a good way to warm up, hot showers.

Wednesday,
November 11, 2009
Thank you Lord Oh Lord, thank you for showing me why I'm here. Goldy is hurting so bad. Please Lord, ease her mind and take away her pain away. She is too sweet for worry. Tell me Lord what to say, and help me to help her like Jesus would. Let me serve you like Jesus would. Let me serve you like Jesus would. Let me serve you Oh Lord. Watch over my children and thank you for blessing me house. Please let all my kids be safe. And Lord, God, thank you for my gifts and abilities to help others. Help me to be stronger and know when to speak and when to keep quiet, and just listen. Yes, Lord, I will do as you say, for I am your servant. I pray in the name of the Father, the Son, and the Holy Ghost. Amen.

I wrote to my girls too. Even though I didn't mail them, it made me feel better just to write to them. I figured that when I got out that they would still be able to read them, to let them know I never forgot about them.
Dear Girls,
I'm ok. I miss y'all too much and love you guys too. This place is like the dumping grounds to leave all your shit behind. I feel like being the mother that you guys deserves.

Love, Mommy

I went to church in jail and soaked up the bible lessons like a sponge. I knew God had a purpose for me. And the volunteers handed out pamphlets. And of course, I would go back to my cell, on my bunk, and write.

November 12, 2009

What The Pamphlet Said:	*My Interpretation:*
Preach the Goodness to the poor	*- Poverty of the soul.*
Heal the Brokenhearted	*- no one understands or cares, heals us.*
Bring Deliverance to the Captives	*- freedom, free me from my old self.*
Give Sight to the Blind	*- those who cannot see His grace.*
Bring Liberty to the Oppressed	*- understand your worries, and hurts; release me from the burdens that's holding me back.*

Dear Lord,
Thank you for keeping me safe, as I take refuge in your arms.

Still November 12, 2009: Thursday
Dear God,
Thank you for me not thinking negative with your help. I want to do what's right and I feel so teachable. Help me while I'm here, help me through another day. Help me to help someone else. Tell me and show me how to express my gifts. And I write in the name of the Father, the Son, and the Holy Spirit. Amen.

Monday: November 16, 2009:
It's about 2:30 and I feel okay. Don't know if I'm going to get any canteen, so I guess I can feel ok. Anyway, I can't believe, I can just a little, love. Thanks for loving me always. I'm at your mercy too. Guide me and let me serve you. Show me the way. In the name of the Father, the Son, and the Holy Spirit. Amen.

Sunday: November 22, 2009:
We went outside today and I felt a little relief. A shining light that never goes out, reckon'n God's word. I feel so hungry, at times as all kinds of foods run thru my mind.

Still the 22nd:
One more day to go. And deep down inside, I'm ready, cause when you need to stay and you wanna go, you must stay. And when you want to stay, and you need to go, then you must go. So, I guess I'm ready. I never want to get too comfortable here. I learn a lot. It's been a challenge. I feel so close to God. I love the Lord so much. How much my faith has grown. Please forgive me as I surrender to you always. I love you, I love me and my family. Amen.

88

Repeating Cycles. Again.
Part 2

The rest of 2009 wasn't much different. Nothing much had changed. After I gotten out of the stockade, we moved out of Jack's place and went to downtown WPB. My 2 girls and I, with my son being out of the service and my oldest daughter completing Job Corp successfully, we had enough to move. Things were going to get better and yet the worst was still yet to come. I didn't think things could get any worse.

Both of my girls had jobs and I cleaned houses. I kept a hold of things the best I could. They once told me that in rehab that I could never really get high again once you become aware of what drug addiction is. Of course, I didn't believe that. I was determined to prove that to be wrong. So, I tested the waters and managed to mess things up again. I was even deeper into my addiction. My daughters told me, "Ma, you need to go back to treatment." And I promised them and God, I can do this without going back because I had all the tools, I needed from the last time I was there. I was just going to apply them this time. I told them I was going to detox again and this time I would stick to the program, and go to the meetings. I just needed a few days of being clean, and I would be 'F.I.N.E." ("Feelings Inside Not Expressed")

Detox became a cycle. Repeating over and over. There were times I couldn't even get a bed. So, to prevent getting sick, I had no choice but to use. And so the circle became unbroken. Almost every time I left detox, no matter what, I eventually used again. Sometimes I would leave before my time was up. Because all I needed was a few days without using and I'd get myself together. But that never seemed to happen as I planned. I was very successful at relapsing. That was the one thing I was really good at. And I seemed to have never failed. Jail couldn't seem to keep me clean and I had gotten picked up for the last time, or so I thought.

I had gotten out of jail again, in our new apartment that we had for a few months, and my oldest daughter told me she was moving out since I didn't want to get better. I didn't believe that she'd move. And then one day she gave me an ultimatum. She told me either go back to treatment in residence for 60 days or she would never speak to me again. I tried to explain to her why I couldn't. Who would watch her little sister? And she immediately told me, "I will. You're neva home anyways. Hell, I'd been doing it." She had gotten another apartment to get away from me. And since I didn't stop, she took her sister with her. That began the start of my breaking point.

I remember the day so clearly. She was gathering all her stuff up and she moved out with one move. I told her I'd be alright. I just needed to move out of here and I'd go to treatment. But I didn't know when. She very clearly told me she wouldn't be in my life until I got out of a drug treatment program. Her were last words were, *"Call me when you're ready ma."* She kissed me on my cheek, looked back at me and gently shut the door. I will never forget that look on her face and the rejected, abandoned feeling that dwelled within me, passed in my stomach to my knees. I couldn't get up to even go after her cause I had no feeling in my legs. And I would have surely fallen on my face. As I look back now, I had hurt my daughter tremendously and I am happy to say today she is still in my life and we're as close as a mother and daughter can be considering all I put her through. She tells me she's proud of me and takes my advice when I'm asked. Today I can be the mother she needs and she is my daughter I never want those lines to be blurred again. I am also happy to say she's a brave woman that will speak her mind with truth and love.

Chapt. 14 - Ready For A Change
Part 1

We were in a new year anyway. I went back to drug treatment to the same place, second time seven years later. I had gotten so old looking and had lost so much weight. I hated myself. I hated what I had did to my kids. I just wanted the pain to stop. When my oldest daughter left that day, she had the saddest look on her face, in her eyes. And the way she shut the door. That will be something I will never forget. When she pulled the door shut to a close, turning back to look at me, with eyes full of tears, yet they didn't fall, I knew I had broken her heart and my heart was torn up too. Somehow, I knew I had been in bad shape that I had ever been up until this point. What could I do to fix it? Just the thought of her not being in my life until I was clean and working a program seemed all too complicated. She came back from time to time to check on me and I wouldn't look at her. She said, "Ma, call me when you're ready to go to treatment. I'll make sure you'll get there." Because I couldn't stay in the apartment cause the rent wasn't paid, I knew it was a matter of time but I wasn't ready to make a date to the depart from this residence downtown. I would always tell her," I'll do it on Monday." It was weird, I didn't even know what day it was. I just always said, "Monday."

Many Mondays came and went. But somehow, I couldn't get those eyes of hers out of my mind. So eventually the time came when I had all I could bear. The pain, torture, and torment of self-sabotaging myself had to come to an end. So I put myself back in rehab. In class that day our instructor, who overcame alcohol, always told us, "to keep it green." "We must always remember the pain and how our family had been affected." That's how I came to write "*Saddened Eyes*." Still, little did I know by writing this poem about describing how my daughter's eyes looked, it would always take me back to the moment of clarity. And whenever I felt like leaving or things weren't going right in treatment, I would reflect back on "*Saddened Eyes*." This was all I needed to spot check myself and keep the pain fresh.

Saddened Eyes

"At half-mast- with the saddest eyes I had ever met."
"Whose eyes I'll never forget."

When I feel down and out and I feel like it's too hard,
I think back, my memory puts me to the test,
To think back to her teary eyes, filled at half mast, slanted like Chinese
It drops me like it's hot, it brings me to my knees.

It brings back the moment, my moment of despair,
It brings me back to my past, when I didn't even care
I didn't want to live no more.
I feel her pain, those sadden eyes, it breaks me to my core.
Take me back to that day when she slowly gazed at me

While slowly walking out the door.

I watched her eyes, I felt her pain,
Yet she never shed a tear,
Remembering being all alone, by myself
Feeling many fears.
Never will I ever forget, my daughter with the saddest eyes you'd ever seen
That gave me a reason to seek help, a desperation; A memory to stay clean.

By Morning Star Of God

Sadden Eyes - *"A sign of a broken heart.*
Her eyes mourn the pain I felt. And her pain was that she was helpless. Therefore, my love for her, she knew all too well. She had to leave me, her heart broken, so I could be fixed. The pain and the hurt, and the sorrow, struck me thru those eyes of hers."

After this, it was now that I was able to put into words what actually happened to me in 2005. When I was stuck between heaven and hell. I wrote this right after "Saddened Eyes." A scene from my dreadful past. I was very lost and in a lot of pain. This is how I felt, like an angel without a face. I actually did this. I went to hell. I was in the split division of my torturous emotions that broke me with the spiritual warfare of what's good and evil. And where did I fit in? I didn't know. I believed at that moment, I was stuck in limbo, somewhere between a heavenly paradise and the pits of a damnation of hell.

> "REGRETFULLY THE DAYLIGHT CAME, THEY SEE ME AS I DECAY, HOPING NO ONE SEE'S ME, KNOW ONE KNOWS, JUST CAN'T SEEM TO LET GO"

Heaven Or Hell

The sky parted, and clouds gave way, while driving
down the road I drove today.
As I fastly falled, I stared in awe!
Much too much to my dismay… (In limbo) in a trance I went
And there I stayed.
  Heaven or Hell, Hell, I can't tell,
I musta slipped, slipped and fell.

And now all the pain, the sorrow so intense, intense.
  Remains, Remains! 'Cause when I got the chance
I never changed.
  Now I done gone crazy, done went insane
  And the sad part about it, was…
 the pain, the shame, the blame.
I only got worse, stayin' the same.
  Still my pattern, my cycle repeats, repeats…
My own damn fault, my own defeat…….
  …. Slowly… I came around
My mind so haunted, with visions of my slow death
My mind taunted… of this place to where I've fallen,
As if to be in another dimension?
  Not to speak of, not to mention,
The dusty, musty smell
  As I come to realize, as you can tell…
  I'm not dead,
  Not dying,
  But living like a prisoner
  In my own damnation
  In my own damn HELL!!
      By Tina Lopez

Keeping It Moving
Part 2

After being in treatment for about 45 days, I had to see my therapist once a week. Her job was to check my progress of how much I was changing. And since my middle name was 'relapse,' she was on me all the time. My therapist was a former heroin addict turned drug therapist. She used to tell me that I reminded herself of me, how she used to be. I wasn't sure how to take that. But I believe she saw something in me that I couldn't see.

One day I remember I walked into her office and she said, "When?" "When!?" "When!!??" "When are you going to get enough? Are you done yet?" I looked at her surprised at this question. Like who does she think she is. Without giving her an answer, I walked out. I heard her saying, "Don't slam my door neither!" I was stuck, had I made reservations and didn't know it? Immediately I said, "No." At this time, all I could do was pray and write. So immediately, I began writing out my prayers. I believed I was done. I believed I had enough. All I could do at this time to the best of my ability is write out my prayers, like I always did, and pray about the situation and our one-sided conversation that took place. I couldn't believe my therapist. I couldn't even get one-word in. I thought, "I'll show them. I'll show them all. I'll never use drugs again. I got this." Complacency and overconfidence had already started forming within me. And she saw that.

September 25, 2010

Gift of Prayer

I want to write a poem
But I don't know what to say.

I pray to God for His blessings
every night, noon, and day.

Today He wants me to write,
about the feelings I seem
To stuff inside

Asking Him to let the angels sit
on my shoulders,
and they never tell me lies.
I write of love, forgiveness
and hope,

I write to God and thanking Him
For getting me off dope.
But most of all I write,
To the person I want

to spend my eternal life with,

My One, My Jesus, God,
Who gave me this?
Wonderful writing gift.
Amen.
                    Netanis L.H.

After I wrote "*The Gift of Prayer,*" I went back for a moment of clarity and read "*Saddened Eyes*" to myself again. I believed at that time I was done. So, I wrote this.

October 18, 2010

When Do I Begin?

"When is enough enough?"
Mystery of captive
At once to disguise
Shameful lust
With seeing eyes

Expressed to love
Beauty turns ashes
Destroying all hope
And my life back flashes

Ruins turns decay
No one else dares
Profound no truth
Claim no cares

All mourn 'er fate
Such weak mortal self
Conducting a pattern
Where pain is felt

Death is a corpse
You life ends
Time moves swiftly
Is to live, when?
Today I begin.

                    Tina L

I had made up my mind, I was going to do this right, this time. Just before Thanksgiving, I got out of treatment that year. My daughters saved their money and got a place together. They will be having a celebration that I'm clean for the holiday and giving thanks to God. But there was a stipulation. I had to go to a halfway house. I wasn't permitted to live with them until I was six months clean. That hurt me but if that's what it took, then so be it.

My daughters, my therapists, and my support group was right. I was going to relapse again because I jumped into a relationship with a guy I met on the men's side of the halfway house. The rules were to stay out of relationships, don't go into our old stomping grounds, and stay away from old negative so-called friends. I broke all those rules and some more. You know people, places and things, it's true. You will relapse if you don't listen.

I moved in with him just before Christmas that year. By the New Year, I was using again and he was back in jail. This time I was again, alone, scared and fearful. It was like I picked up right from where I left off at. He ended up with charges VOP and was sentenced to six years in prison. So once again, I checked out. The only good thing that ever happened as the year rolled on, 2011, was the birth of my first grandchild. By that time, both of the girls lived with me in the apartment that my boyfriend and I had occupied. God seems to take people out of your life that you don't really need somehow. What I thought was God going against me by taking people out of my life just when I thought I was happy, turned out to be a blessing in disguise that I failed to see, until it was too late. Immediately, I did the only thing I knew that would take my pain away. No wonder they say, "Do not get into relationships for the first year of recovery." I felt defeated, like a failure. I had loved and lost again and convinced myself that I would always be a loser. Not knowing the enemy like I do today, that was the devil telling me that and I played right into 'its' hand. Not today because I know the TRUTH and the power of the Lord that lives in me.

I was present for the birth of my grandchild and I thought, now I have a reason to live and do right.   But what I learned was if I didn't stay clean for myself, it wouldn't work. I can say that this time, I really realized that I didn't love myself. The old saying goes, "If you don't love yourself, how you going to love somebody else?"

In the middle of May exactly, my first grandchild was born. Later that same year, I was back in jail, moved again and the cycle continued and a new year was beginning. All I could do was pray now being back in familiar ground. Surviving became my way of life in the streets. I didn't write no more for a while and said my prayers aloud while I walked down the streets.

Chapt.15 - Undercover Lover?

I found myself once again waking up in jail. Not remembering how I really got there, nor was I caring. But as I woke up and prayed, thanking God that I was still alive. Then I remembered how I got here. I was in a sting. I was here to stay for fifteen days. So, I made the most and the best of it. I wrote to make myself, to make myself laugh and the other girls and wrote *You Know You're In Jail When...*

Sept 12, 2011

You Know When You're In Jail......Too Long....

When... You've gained 12 pounds in 5 days.
When ... Your bunkie starts looking inviting and ya not gay.
When ... the only thing worse than jail has to be death by strangulation
When.... Suddenly you can draw, brings out hidden talents, you just know
> *you're an artist or something.*
When... A girl starts singing and that shit sounds good.
When... When something as a small as a jolly rancher that you have to
> *share (cause she's staring) tastes so good, and you Thank God*
> *cause it tastes so good*

When... all you have to look forward to is eating that nasty food
When... You wake up looking like death warmed over, and all you been
> *is sleeping for a week, getting your beauty rest*
When...You are freezing seconds upon arrival
When...Your friend say they saw you in the paper (so smile)
When...Steel seats never warm up no matter how much you blow ya hot
> *breath on it.*
When...You see your friend that's been missing for a minute that you just
> *got high with last week and she's in jail for the same charges you*
> *are.*

I thought *This is crazy. Are you 'effin kiddin me?* Waking up in jail for the third time this year was my reality. My first thought was remembering the firm words of the last time I saw the judge. *"Miss Lopez, if you come before my chambers again, you will be habitualized. That will be a felony charge placed against you, which includes prison time."* Since I wasn't processed in a timely manner, I missed first appearance. There was a lot of us caught in that sting that day. We even made the news. Oh boy I thought. 'My goose is cooked.' There's no getting out of this one. So, I did what I always did. But this time I cried real tears to God. I thought about my kids, instead of thinking about myself, I was asking myself, who's going to take care of my kids now? So, I got down on my knees by my bunk and didn't care who was looking. I asked for His mercy. I asked if He could get me out of this, promising that if I only had one more chance to make this right, I would do whatever you ask me to. So, this is what happened.

God is the only one who can make a way out of a no way situation. And that's exactly what He did. Because I missed first appearance, the judges changed shift. For the first time they started a new reform program that day. It so happened to be for all us girls that got caught up in the sting. That program was run by a woman judge that I will be facing for this case.

It was a program to get hustlers off the street with drug problems and making them a responsible member of the community and society. The public thought we were all menaces. With the tourist season coming back and all the snowbirds, they wanted to "sweep the streets." That was the reason for the sting operation. Since I was a lady of the evening and a drug user that would be me. I was informed that if I signed papers agreeing to this there would be no jail time.

Mr. Reform would be picking me up and having an interview. In that interview, he asked me what I needed to do to make myself a better person. Of course, I said, "I used drugs but being in here locked up, I had a chance to clean up." He believed me and I believed me too. I was so sincere. All I needed to get right was a place for my grandchild and two daughters. Of course, there were rules for every program. Rule #1 - I must go to meetings. Rule #2 - I must meet with a counselor each week. Rule #3- I must take random drug test. Rule #4- I can't catch no new charges.

With all that being said, Mr. Reform found us a place. It was a two-bedroom apartment with washer and dryer and all the bills were paid. I guess you could say I was in transition. The goal was to get a job, be self-sufficient, and live like a normal person. You know it's funny how quickly we forget. My sick thinking told me now you've got it made for real. No bills, roof over our head and free meals for everyone. But one thing was missing. I had a craving to escape what I was feeling. I couldn't sleep. So, I found the only quick cure that I knew. While in jail, I learned about a certain opiate called 'blues' or 'Roxy's.' I learned that was the new heroin and where to find it if I needed it.

It wasn't long at all before I was back out there again. One taste of this new drug and I was hooked, lured, line and sinker. Off to the races I went. With the New Year approaching, not much changed with me. I ended up back in jail on another soliciting charge in another district. The undercover let me go with a court dated ticket. But when the time came for court, I ended up doing time. I was caught in the sting from the first time plus new charges. By the beginning of the New Year, we were forced out of the apartment the program provided for us by fire.

I think back now on how God's grace was always there for me. We all escaped the electrical fire that day. The aftermath could have turned out tragic. This is one of the times during the writing of my book when I talked about how God saved me more times than I would like to remember. Because I have been known to over think myself into a frenzy, It worked out good for me not to have graphic memories of what could have been. My mother used to tell me when I

98

would call her, "honey stop letting your mind roam of what's not really happening and if you can't stop your over imagination self, girl put it in a fiction book."

Now in the present day I take heed to her advice she gave me a long time ago. In the books to come that I will write will be fiction no doubt, based on actual events. In my great mind of creativity, my mental artistic agility and the reality of what could have been of my conclusions, from past experiences of my fantasy and wild delusions on how I once perceived my life through the darkness until the light shined upon me which would be many more years to come like in the Word: *John 14:6 (NIV): "Jesus answered, "I am the way and the truth and the life. No one comes to the Father except through me.*

"If you are the problem, you can't go to yourself for the solution."

Chapt.16 – Cotton Fevers

Part 1

By that time, my oldest daughter had already gotten her own place on 31st, downtown, West Palm Beach. So, we all moved in with my daughter. And my oldest became pregnant with twins. I relapsed again. Extremely into total darkness. I got money the best way I knew how, hustling, selling drugs, cleaning houses by any means necessary. No more writing. Every now and then I would journal. Not long after moving in, I went to jail again. I missed the birth of the twins being born. Talk about feeling bad about myself. I deserved this. Instead of having any felony charges, they sentenced me to eighteen days. From the charges I received last year and some more new ones once again I woke up in regret. This time there would no first appearance, no going in front of the judge. I was dope sick for about five days. And they medicated me. Once again, I reached out to God. All I could do was pray and hope that everything went well with my daughter's delivery. I felt so guilty. I couldn't even be there for their own birth. Again, I did the only thing I knew, I reached out to God for answers.

April 14, 2012

Dear Father, My Father, (so unfinished and uncorrected)
Today I feel so distressed. For I have not no money. I have not freedom...etc. My life a waste, my life a mess. Such a mess.
Then today I began to cry. For I longed for my family. And I begged to know Lord, why? Why me, why? So, I sat so still, filled with gloom. And very quiet about this very dark room.
A voice spoke so firm, yet so distinct, as I remember to think. "My child, you weep,
so sad, I know you feel so bad. 'Ya ask me a question, tis not to be forgotten? Why has this life you led so terrible distraught, you fight it and fought an addiction so horrible be true. Because I choose to do. Question me not, but why not you?

Dear God, April 29, 2012
Thank you for waking me up in jail. Thank you for delivering me through my hard times and sorrows. And Lord today, I know I can't do anything without you. Please restore my health and sharpen my mind. Rejuvenate my body and hair. Let my skin show my heart. God, I ask that you lead me into the right path. Help me to find a job. Jesus don't let me go astray. Lord you know my heart and you know what I need, when I need it. Tonight, I will not worry and put my hands in yours. And I will do your will. Father God, bless over all the women here and deliver them when you see fit. Let them go home to their families and children. Let them cry no more and let them not return. God, I love you so much cause you always know what I need when I need it. And I have faith by your undying love for me, your grace, you will find a way for me. I love you God. Thank you for sending your only son Jesus Christ, to die for our sins. I write to you with so much love and sing your praises. Lord, I will never forget who you are. In my heart, I always thank you for making me a writer, a poet, a storyteller. And God show me what I feel. Let me realize what I must write about. Help me

to write my feelings down. Show me the way to go. As the night falls into another day, bless me Oh Lord, with the truth of the sweetest dreams. In the name of the Father, Son, Holy Ghost. In Jesus' Name, Amen.

Dear God   *April 30, 2012*
      Lunch is coming. Thank you, God. I feel great that I can write me fears away. It does get better. And I am feeling okay. An okay is a feeling. I'm waiting on lunch and I think everything will be alright. Right now, I am feeling left out, rejected, and out casted. And not worthy of. Is that my disease striking? All this arguing over food is so petty. God, get me into a positive mood. Okay?

1. *I'm clean*
2. *Grandkids*
3. *May 7th*
4. *The positive girls*
5. *3 meals*
6. *Getting better*
7. *Have a plan*
8. *I can write with gift*
9. *Motivated*
10. *God always looks out*

    Lunch is coming and I'll stay to myself. I see so much greediness. I don't want to be like that. It's rainy today and I like that. I was feeling better.

      Dear God,
      Thank you for letting me write again. Please help me keep my mind open and my heart full of your grace. Lord, thank you for Kim. Cause she died and I was thinking of her and my disease. She is reminding me of my disease. Lord I will accept wherever you send me. I love you so much. I ask you to continue to watch over my kids and their small babies. Please help me take away my cravings of drugs and my desire to use again. Thank you for today. And although I struggle from time to time, I know you always have my back. Thank you for letting me get my thoughts out and my feelings that still blog my mind. I'm feeding into the negativities. I'm glamorizing about 'tricks.' I feel like that sometimes. I be disappointing my own self. But I do know it's a learning process. By journaling I feel better now, as I wait for dinner. As I know this day is almost over. Help me Lord to help myself stay in today. Help me to say the words to run the women's group meeting tonight.

    So many thoughts would race through my head. So I wrote it poetically. This is what I wrote:

> *As I lay in bed*
> *All kind of thoughts*
> *Linger in my head.*
>
> *Thoughts of what coulda been,*
> *& "I shoulda."*
> *& what "woulda."*
> *I have regrets, of days gone by,*
> *Guilty,*
>
> *Many lingering thoughts in my head*
> *How my life's has gone astray*

102

Tossing & turning in my bed.
Wish they'd all just go away.

Questioning myself again & again, over & over
'Bout how different my life coulda been,
Constantly looking for troll over, my shoulder
Losing a battle, I'll never win.

Realizing in this place that maybe its
Not too late,
And my everything could change
Wanting to leave, & try can't wait
Not wanting to be
The same

So, I guess I have to be positive
In everything I do.
And they say stick with God
It will come true.

Learning to love myself, is a
Battle so brand new. Thoughts of what "can't be, "

'Krap' my pencil is worn down and I won't be able to write.'

But I did manage to find a scrawny looking jailhouse pen that was running out of ink, just like me, running out of hope. I wasn't looking forward to the day of my release cause I got much in store for me and I needed a rest. So I wrote:

Never smile. Hungry. Meanwhile – Abuse
What's the use?
Too late. Delete.
Contemplate. Wrong –
Too long.
Can't go home
Streets, everywhere, roam, you roam.
So messed up,
Want change
Rearrange
My life
Think twice
It's insane
Do the same
When nothing changes (guess what?)
Nothing changes.
Steal.
Trick.
Deal.

Sick.
Sleep – the repeats – as you awake
Sick.
Gotta work.
Trick.
Herk & Jerk.
Nothing works.

So the time went by and I went home, not knowing that the next time what laid ahead of me on my next return to jail, would be almost my last day I live. Since my disease of addiction was getting way out of hand, I remembered reading in the Bible about every time you relapse. It said you pick up more and more demons each time. I didn't understand this but this was exactly what was happening to me!

Matthew 12:45 Then the spirit finds seven other spirits more evil than itself, and they all enter the person and live there. And so that person is worse off than before. That will be the experience of this evil generation." NLT – Boy, talk about those generational curses and spirits that are passed down into our families. It's actually a fact I have come to believe cause it actually happened to me. I must break this cycle. I did this with a lot of prayer, confidence and faith in Jesus Christ.

And I'm Back. "Old Habits Die Hard"
Part 2

"Guess what folks? Guess where I'm at? Back in jail." All that talk I did and all that praying I did. I believed my own lies. At the time I didn't seem like I was lying to myself. Soon as I walk across that cat walk, the enemy was waiting in the parking lot. Right on the police compound. There 'John' sits. Catching girls that are so vulnerable and there I went.

WOW!!! Like I said before, *you keep doing what you always done, you gonna keep getting what you always get.* And so, I'm back again. So, I do what I've always done when you don't have a choice and how my life looks so drab, so I reached out to God for the countless time.

November 19, 2012.

For some reason, it seems like I just left the place.

Dear God   *November 20, 2012*

Another day at the county jail and I'm okay. I feel not the decency to mess up but only to do what's right. I tried to call my kids, no answer. Anyway, I love them just the same. And I was disappointed but just the same, I'll get over it.

November 21, 2012

Please remove all my shortcomings and blessed be the day I walk out on the catwalk helping me not to forget all of my sorrows of drugs. About to go to sleep. It's 9:30.
'

November 22, 2012

Oh Lord what's to happen? I can't even fathom what just lied ahead of me this morning. At the hospital and I'm still alive. What happened? I ask myself over & over. In jail and I still found some way, not even on purpose to hurt myself. I don't know what else to say, really what else to feel so I turn to You Lord, once more. In time I'm so troubled, I call on You. I'm hurt. So very hurt. How can I turn my negative into a positive? Help me God, for I have sinned and fallen short of the day once again. Once again, my life is possible only thru you. I know you have 'preparest a table for me and thank you Lord, for not inviting me at this time. I think how life can really be stopped unexpectedly on accident on accident and I never saw it coming. My life was spared and I'm going to take this episode and run with it. Something has traumatized me and something is just different. Something just is! God I am so grateful for being alive I'm grateful for sitting in the county jail today and even though I go home tomorrow I've never felt better in my life and I'm willing to do whatever it is to make this right I write I pray in the name of the father and of your son and of the Holy Ghost. Amen

Dear Jesus,
How I've fallen and once again and always You, it's You who love me and not condemn me, for this I can be truly blessed. Amen.

I believed I was finished. I was tired and this revolving door of jail wasn't getting any easier. I sat down in my bunk and I wrote:

I WANNA DO RIGHT

I want to do right
Cuz I'm tired of doing wrong.
I want to do right
Cuz I've been rong too long.
I want to do right
Cuz I can't take the pain.
I want to do right
Cuz I'm ready for a change.
So, I sit and pray
And I realize I made it
Clean thru another day.
And I'm gonna to do right
Cuz it's what's in my heart
And I'm gonna to do right
Today is the first start.

Dear God,   *November 23, 2012*
Thank you, God, for today. Just realized my son's birthday was yesterday and my baby boy is 24. Thank you for my kids. This morning I love you so much unlike any other morning. Thank you, Lord, for letting me live again. I asked you that you watch over here and leave this place today. Something feels so different today please don't let me snapback into activated addiction. Lord it is so cunning, baffling and powerful but you are more powerful than that. Today Lord about to you too feel you and fulfill my heart with faith. What is you Lord restores my mind my heart and my soul. Amen

That evening, after I finished writing my prayer, the weekenders came in. There was a girl that brought in contraband. She had been bringing pills in on her weekends. All the other inmates, including myself, knew what was going on. She had to bring enough in for them too to keep their mouths shut. If she didn't, they act stank to her and this particular night, she didn't give them any. And because of this, they told. And like jealous snitches do, they informed the deputies on duty that night. So, with the deputies having a heads up, they were watching her closely that night when she came in. It all happened so fast. The
106

deputies rushed up the fire exit to catch her in the act. I saw everything going down. Right when they pushed the door open, she threw a napkin balled up on my bed. With my quick reactions, I just grabbed it without thinking as they shouted for all of us to get on the ground. I shoved the napkin into my mouth and while they were escorting her out, I drank from the water fountain to swallow the evidence. I thought, "Shoot. I'm going home tomorrow. When they're not looking, I'll throw it up. They ain't gonna catch me with this stuff. I ain't gonna catch no charges for nobody."

This is what actually happened. One of the girls told that I put something in my pocket. So they led me into this room. Stripped search and cavity searched me too. They didn't find anything. Of course, they didn't, it was in my belly. But the thing was, the pills were dissolving and they kept staring at me through the glass. I started getting so dizzy and seeing black spots before my eyes. All I wanted to do was go to sleep and close my eyes. But the coldness of the jail cell kept me awake. Almost an hour had passed by before they decided to let me out of the room. By this time, I was incoherent and uncoordinated. I mean, I couldn't even walk. I stumbled all over the place. Then one of the sheriff deputies noticed something just wasn't right. I remember her asking me if I knew where I was. I replied, "Yes. I'm in a daycare center." I heard her snicker as she asked for help to usher me down into medical. And to get an ambulance in route because I was overdosing. She asked me what I swallowed. I told her it was Ambien. I think I had swallowed twelve or thirteen of them. I was rushed to the nearest hospital where they pumped my stomach, handcuffed me to the rail to the hospital bed and I was watched by two male deputies that even stayed in the room with me. When I woke up, a doctor was standing over me, asking me did I know what day it was. He told me if that I ate, I could be released. I was released about 5:30 in the morning.

I was back at the county. I saw a look of relief on the guard's face. The jail nurse told me that I almost died. I should have never swallowed the pills. I should have told the guards what I did right from the start. And as I went to thank her, she said, "Don't thank me, thank God. You got somebody watching over you." And I was then escorted back to my bunk in my cell. All the deputies on duty that night, let them know that I scared them. I was really trying to process what happened. To make a long story short, God's grace in abundance had saved me from my accidental mistakes, once again.

When I got home, I was in for a rude awakening. I was no longer welcome there. My daughters were hurt, embarrassed and mad. And I couldn't blame them. Hell, I was mad at my damn self. I got what little stuff I had and I moved in with a drug dealer. I thought that would make things easier for me. I swore I would never go to jail again on those charges again and nor would I never spend another night in jail again. And I didn't.

At Dude's house I have my own room, as long as I worked for him. All would be well. I felt safe there for the first time in a while. Working for 'Dude,' I managed to save up '7 stacks plus'. I made sure my kids have money all the time and I thought I was doing pretty good. My lil' girl and my grandson were moving out into their own place. I was asked to move in with them too. I enrolled myself in college and brought the New Year in changing my ways. I was still using but I looked at it as my "*medicine*." I was really trapped in this prison of drug addiction and I had no choice but to use. I couldn't function without it. I mean when I tell you that I could not do squat. I wasn't good for *nuthn*. I accepted this as becoming my new way of life. Like food shelter and water in order to survive, I was different I needed more like opiates to go about my days like a normal person. Opiates, controlled, every aspect of my whole life and my being.

Chapt.17 - Broken Hearts Do Mend
Part 1

It wasn't long after I moved out that Dude got busted. I knew it was just a matter of time. There was so much more that happened there during that time. It was a safe way to make money with men besides going out on the street. What they call today "human sex trafficking". In which I am not going to go into detail about what happened in this book for my own personal reasons. However, what I will say is I was very vulnerable from being on very addicted drugs during the opioids epidemic and I played into a trap of cohesion along with misleading blinding ambitions ending with false results. It will be known in the future as my untold stories.

With the money I had managed to save while working for 'Dude' previously, I used it to enroll in college. I signed up to be a drug counselor because that's what I knew real good. But first I must pay them. I owed them my financial obligations from previous years of going to school. Since I had money, I made my financial amends, paid it, enrolled. And I thought I had it made. I thought, I got this. I guess I got a little complacent. Well truth be told; I got a whole lot complacent.

And it wasn't long before I was paranoid, frail and wretched. I guess it's what they call it in the streets 'tore down'. I started having fevers again. This time they were coming back to back. I couldn't seem to catch a break. I just thought it was strep throat. My lil' girl had just gotten over it. So, I thought, I must have caught it since I was susceptible to it having had it many times in the past as a child.

Never did the thought occur to me that it was the drugs and the old my way of me and my thinking. Also never did the thought cross my mind that even though I wasn't out there in the streets anymore and enrolled in college that I couldn't fail. I really thought I had a handle on this. I had money, my kids didn't go without, the bills were paid. Such denial I seemed to be in but I still couldn't see it. That just goes to show you what they say is true. Just how cunning, baffling and powerful the disease of addiction really is.

I didn't know what was going to take for me to stop. I cried out to God, *"I can't do this anymore Lord."* But I didn't know how to stop. I mean I could stop but I couldn't stay stopped. I started getting fevers again and this time they were more frequent than usual. So in another attempt of desperation, I cried out to God for help as I did so many times in the past. But this time, my grandson woke up my daughter and called 911. This happened in June 2013. That stay in the hospital cost me to drop out of college that I just started, the use of my legs and 3 months in the hospital. And I also missed out on making fast money for Dude. *Like are you friggin' kidding me? What am I thinking? How warped is my thinking?* Looking back, I was a very sick individual.

I had left the hospital in a wheelchair. I couldn't bend my knees due to being septic. Doctors, they had to put drains in them and then cut them open to flush out the infection. I ended up with Endocarditis for the second time. I was told my aortic valve was infected. They would have to do surgery. There was no time to waste. By morning I was referred to a heart hospital. I was given a tissue replacement heart valve which was a pig's intestines. I had indeed infected it again. This time I thought I would surely die. But I didn't. I was so self-centered. God saved me from myself once again. By now I had really lost count. *Again!!*

......

I was released in August of that year only to return to the hospital with terrible, severe headaches and more fevers. Ambulance was called again. This time my diagnosis was spinal meningitis. They had caught it early and I was given antibiotics for the 3 weeks. During this time, I had learned how to use a walker. And I made the most out of it. I was determined to walk. I had to stand strong and believe for I was given another chance. This was not supposed to be like this. I was told before I left that I was just 'lucky'. "No, I wasn't!" I exclaimed. "I am His favorite." Before this year was out, I walked again with a slight limp. I got besides myself and so the story goes. I ended up back in the hospital and forgot about going back to college. I broke my promise to God, my children and to myself. Again, I was killing myself slowly. I felt all I needed was strength. I wanted to walk again like a normal person like I used to be. Today it reminds me of the scripture ***Isaiah 40:31 NKV: But they that wait upon the Lord shall renew their strength; they shall mount up with wings as eagles; they shall run, and not be weary; and they shall walk, and not faint.*** Like who knew the last words of this verse would come to my mind in the next three years to come?

I did learn to walk again. I gained my strength back. And then I forgot about my promises to Jesus. In no time I used again. My sick thinking told me *Girl, you fixed now. Now you can really use. It ain't gonna happen again. Just keep your needles brand new. And your sites clean.* And that's what I did for a while. It seemed to work for a while, a short while. Within a year I was back, sicker than a dog.

"Just keep on, keep on doing what you've always done, just keep on, ya gonna keep getting what you always get. Duh."
"When am I ever going to learn?"

Chapt.18 - It Was Almost A Year To The Date

     Almost a year to date that I got sick with my heart valve. And I was infected with Endocarditis for the third time. I really convinced the doctors that I won't use again the last time I was in the hospital. I convinced myself and I meant it at the time. I really couldn't grasp the concept that it wasn't the drugs, it was me. I had a lot of hurt and pain. I was mad at the world. I was not mad at everyone that had hurt me. And still, I couldn't understand it. I thought with surgery with the tissue valve, I was fixed. The old heart valve parts were gone. I thought I couldn't get sick no more. *Just keep on doing what you've always done, ya gonna keep getting what you always get.* Duh.

     Back in the hospital again. I couldn't believe it. I was so damn sick of this place. And they were just as tired of seeing me too. My mind reflected on the words of my physician told me about having Endocarditis. The first time is with antibiotics, second surgery and the third time the body usually won't hold up for surgery. He explained that those patients usually go into a terminally ill facility, like hospice or are sent home to die. I was so disappointed with me. I didn't know much at that time but one thing I did know that I didn't want to die. I was not finished living. I had not finished my book. What I didn't know at the time that everything happens for a reason. God knows my heart. I wanted to live.

     This time in the hospital was different. Doctors said my kidneys were in bad shape. I was in renal and heart failure at the same time. Things were not looking too good for me. I was so swelled up everywhere. My cardiologist came into the room. He had this look on his face of total defeat. He didn't have to say nothing. I already knew what he was going to say. Before he spoke, I uttered, with a harsh voice, "How long do I have?" He said to me, "Less than 30 days." I burst into uncontrollable tears. Just then my mom and my sister walked in the room. I surely was not ready to call it quits.

     My mom held me close and my sister consoled me best she could. Cardiologist returned to tell me that he's going to talk to the heart surgeon again and see what he thinks. Since the surgeon already knew my anatomy from the train accident and the previous heart valve surgery, he would know what he is up against. My numbers had to be right. Potassium, Sodium and my Magnesium had to be a certain level. Or surgery would be useless because I wouldn't even make it off the table.

     So, they gave me hope. About five days later, I returned to the heart hospital to prep for surgery in the early morning. I ended up being intubated for five days before I regain consciousness. What was supposed to be a seven-hour surgery turned to be 12 hours. I was told that doctors had to cut veins out of my calves and my wrist to go into reconstruction of numerous heart valves. In layman's terms, I received a triple bypass heart surgery. A mechanical heart valve was in place of my aortic valve. And it wasn't over yet, before I was released from the hospital, my right lung would fill with fluids and a chest tube

113

was placed to release the fluids. I went into atrial fibrillation, also known as A Fib. But I was still in "dire straits." My body was not responding like they expected. So, days later, a pacemaker was placed in also.

I spent almost four months in the hospital that time. That was the longest I had ever been away from my kids, home and society. Little did I know in the near future, I would almost triple this time. Of course, I wrote when I got a chance. My friend bought me in a journal. I wrote out my prayers thanking God for my life. I felt free at last. I was very grateful to be alive. It was about the only good thing that happened to me. It's then I wrote:

FREEDOM

"As I woke up
A tear sung my eye
I wondered, am I dead?
NO! I did not die."

Thinking in my mind-
Many thoughts came into play.
Be thankful be grateful,
I have lived one more day.
For I didn't want to be here
I'd rather be someplace other,
Be at home, playing with my babies
Being grandmother.

Humbling myself,
I'll get through this the best way I thought.
Thinkin' positively of the past paths
And all the fights I've fought,
That were all my fault.
For now, I can make it through this
With God on my side
To help me see things as they are
For the first time.

And become the woman he wants me to be
By helping others (what took me so long to learn)
Of what I did not know and how I
Let God set me free.
                              Tina L

114

I went home near the end of April of 2014. Things had changed. Both of my daughters had new baby boys. I was happy to return to my new editions of our family but things took a turn with my girls that would send us all in different directions. By Christmas of this year, my oldest moved to Orlando with her boyfriend. And my other daughter was in a domestic violence situation and we all had to relocate. I was ready to go too. Anywhere but here. I had been on the east coast for almost thirty-two years. I was ready to get the heck out of dodge. By this time in my life there seemed to be nowhere in this city that I could go to that wouldn't be a terrible memory of my past that took place. My oldest son came to pack us up with reinforcements (just in case there was trouble) and my lil girl, her 2 boys Joshua and Joel and myself moved to the west coast of Florida. It was here that I thought things would be different. I was right. They were. So different it wasn't long before I was homesick.

This was when we found out that my grandson, Joel was not like a normal baby. It was then that I wrote Broken Wings. Test revealed that he was just a little delayed on his reaching his milestones. Doctors assured he would grow out of it and not to worry, so we didn't. That's how I came to write the poem, not really sharing it with anyone for at least 2 more years. So, Christmas was here. 2014 was almost gone. And I was very homesick for the east coast of Florida. I brought the New Year in with going back to West Palm Beach to say my goodbyes to those that I felt deserved it. This became a pattern every month around the first.

This section of the book is a tribute to Mr. Garvey: One of my dearest friends was an old man named Mr. Garvey.He was a man worthy of his cause. I often (on my quick trips to West Palm) would always stop and check on him and clean his house for him. I would do this because I know he needed the help. Also I just plain right liked the old bugger. He was a wise man. The kind with a little too much sense. He never put me down or criticize me for doing drugs the way I did. However, he often let me know that he believed one day I would give it up and get myself together. Mr.Garvey also loved him some Jesus and the book of Proverbs. He was very secure in his relationship with Him. **Proverbs 29:25 One who trusts in the Lord is secure.** This year in Jan 2020 he passed away.

For Mr. Garvey I am grateful today that he gotten a chance to see me get clean and write my book. I always promised him I would come to his bedside and read it to him because he couldn't see to good due to old age. Last year I took pictures with him, prayed with him and took out to breakfast, my traveling buddy and I. He always ordered the same thing fish and grits with a side of jokes. Today as I proof read my book I read it out loud as if he were here, just to keep my promise I made.

No matter where you go, there you are.

Chapt.19 - Here We Go Again & Again & Again

Part 1

I was getting very depressed and I was starting to isolate myself. I couldn't wait to go back to West Palm Beach. The thoughts in my mind were of my ex-husband and how I felt like he abandoned me. It was like every morning I felt the pain over and over again. All I wanted was the pain stop. The only way I knew of this happening was to escape into my world of feeling where there was no pain. This is what I wrote while waiting on the time to pass by. Every morning as far back in 2000 I felt like this.

August 17, 2015

Every Morning

I awoke this morning and I realize you weren't here.
Not a sound filled the room but my sobbing voice in air.
Knowing that you're not coming back for you nor loved me or cared.
A fact I'll have to face-
When awoken every morning-
To know you're not there.

"Even Though it's been almost two decades since you went away since you've been gone - Every morning I awaken, broken with the torn heart and a sad, sad song."

This is where I realize where the pain really was. It was in my heart and I guess I really was over him. But I wasn't over the situation. I went over in my mind all the things he taught me. When I look back in hindsight, I was taught by one of the best. What I wasn't taught, I figured out by myself. My ex taught me how to be real street smart by using my intuition with wisdom and knowledge to my advantage on how to survive. Besides that, he had moved on a long time ago and was already married again. So, I accepted this again for the last time and moved on. Somehow, I knew that things had to change for me. I always believed that God would help me with this when I was ready. After all the promise I kept to God was to just party until I was 50 and He made sure I kept that promise, holding me to my word.

Going back to West Palm Beach every month became like a bad habit and a pattern that was hard for me shake. I was in such denial. I couldn't even see past my own lies. Justifying, rationalizing and blaming others for my addiction seems easier to deal with. The bottom line was I couldn't face my own reality. I was wretched, lost and broken again. Every month I came back and did the same thing all over and over again, just like all the way up until like August. I was getting older and older and nothing was changing. In August this year I would be 49 years old, and I promised God that I would stop. Things for me seemed so much harder than they ever been. The going back and forth from the east coast to the west coast was tearing me down fast. God's grace had always been there with me but it went unnoticed. Like when I was on the bus coming from West Palm back to Fort Myers this one time, I met a lady that told me about Grace Church and Celebrate Recovery. She planted a seed of going to recovery meetings and where I could find them when I was ready. The thought always stuck with me. It wasn't until January 2017 that I remembered where to go when I got ready. Little did I know, when that day came that I would walk into Grace Church, so grief stricken and desperate for Jesus.

So, you see, you never know what you tell somebody that may not be ready at the time about where to find recovery and a meeting, when it's all really going to sink in. I call them farmers. She planted a seed that day, in 2015 that continues to grow today, as I water the soil. I keep my soil very moist with the thirst for Jesus. I make sure my cup "don't run dry."

To get back to my story, I started getting fevers again. I started staying longer on the east coast and my family just didn't know what to do anymore. Although they never said anything to me, I knew they knew something just wasn't right with me, but at this time nobody could tell me nothing at that time. I wanted what I wanted when I wanted it. You know the typical addict behavior.

Somehow, I always felt like I had to keep in touch my so-called friends that I used with or dealers I worked for. I felt the need to let them know my status. I later learned this was called 'trauma bonding." I was surely making reservations to use again. It was different this time because I didn't do enough to get back hooked but eventually it happened.   I met a neighbor in Fort Myers apartments where I lived at and he had a car. He took a liking to me and I played on his flirtatious gestures. I was all the while planning my next move with using on my mind. He could take me over to the east coast to see my dealer and no one would ever know it, not even my neighbor Warry knew what I was really up to.

Then the day came to make my move. I woke up from a "dope dream" and I had a craving so bad to use. So, I anxiously woke Warry up too, banging and knocking on his window like a deranged crazy lady. Urged him to get up and demanded that we go to WPB. I made up some story about my heart meds that I'm supposed to be taking and that I could only get them in WPB. I drove this time. I didn't care about the police pulling me over I was driving like a maniac. Weaving in and out of traffic speeding, I was determined to get my stuff. How sick was that looking back now. Not even caring about using too soon. Or about the consequences that resulted from when you do.

I knew if I took it this far, I would probably be hooked. And I didn't care. It was better than feeling the pain of the past. Anyone knows that if you use for more than three days in a row, you're hooked. I knew that and still I didn't care. It was too soon to use. Because I used my just the day before. This would be 4 days in a row. Still I didn't care. I told myself to borrow money from Warry and I

118

could get enough to hold me till the first of the month.   I asked, he gave me the money and I was off to the races.

Everything was going according to my plans. I had timed a perfect performance. Until I saw the blue lights in the rearview mirror. Undercover sheriff's deputies had caught me speeding. It was then Warry let me know he didn't have a license nor a valid registration." "Great," I thought. Ain't no way I was going to get out of this one. It was then the deputy came back to the car and told me to step out. My butt was going back to the county jail. The charge would be for driving on a suspended license. And to think I was almost to my destination. That's all I could think about. I swore to myself I would never be back to spend another night in the county jail. *Damit! Damit! Damit! Why did I have to speed? That* was all I could think.

As I look back on my life now God was always with me. He got me out of this one for sure. As it turned out I was booked and released on OR.   My daughter was waiting for me to be released that evening. I proceeded on with my plans to meet up with the 'street pharmacist' and I realized then that I was letting nothing stand in the way of me and my 'medicine.' Nothing!! I was worse and by the time next month came and the court date, I had already been back a couple of more times. My daughter was having her last son and he came early. That was a good excuse to go back before my court date. This time when I went back unknowingly, I would never see another bright day again in the east coast of Florida. Death was near and I was next.

Death Is Here And I am Next
Part 2

I wrote this poem before I left for the birth of my grandson, Kaleb. I had to go back anyway for court and I did what always did but this time was different. I was literally sick and tired. Going back and forth took a toll on me physically. I started getting 'cotton fever' all the time again. I had to use because I couldn't function. Even daily chores of life became a great struggle without the use of synthetic opioids. It was the simplest things couldn't do, like walk to the bathroom, combing my hair even hurt, holding a conversation etc. My time was coming to an end. I felt this in my heart, my spirit and in my soul. I learned that this is what you call being in complete desperation. So, I wrote this to my kids to let them know my drug addiction and my death was not their fault. I loved them and I wanted them to understand that. I knew the time was coming for me to either "shit or get off the pot." I was in total desperation and I was suffocating in my own mess while still alive. I just couldn't take it anymore.

LIFE GOES ON

"The wind blew cool.
The sun hid.
The lake waters ruffled,
As it always did.

The minutes goes slow.
The nights go fast.
The days go on and on,
And seconds last and last."

SO:
-the circle remains unbroken
-and time is repeated
-life is to death
-and life is defeated

THEREFORE:
-I will go to heaven.
-I know I will die.
-it will be a sad day,
when everyone will cry.

HOWEVER:
-Life goes on,
and in goes the sun.
-Night has fallen,
and the ol' day is done.

REMEMBER--
Tomorrow is another day.
A new day has begun.
Just cause I'm dead,
Your lives must continue,
Your lives must go on.

By N. Lopez

Racing Thoughts
Part 3

After writing that last poem of course I was preparing to go to West Palm Beach and I couldn't sleep all night. I was fearing going back to my routine of using because my body was breaking down again and this time, I told God that before I return, I would go back to detox again. I promised never return to West Palm again. See I had a plan. I confessed to God that I had enough, and please forgive me for my wrongs that I've done. My sick patterns repeated over and over. So, when I can't sleep, I write. This would be the last poem that I would write this year. Fooling myself but believing that I was tired of being 'sick and tired'. I wrote my good-bye letter to drugs. In my heart was the desire. I didn't want to do this anymore. So, I wrote:

GOODBYE DRUGS- GOOD RIDDANCE-FAREWELL

Today I morn
Today I grieve
Now your gone, I feel deceived
I miss you so much
My life stinks,
And I can't get up
Without you, I think.

My life the blahs, and
How my heart sinks,
It really sinks.

I know I will see
You again, when we
Will be happy
Life will be brand new
Snappy, snappy.
Then you will leave
Like you always do
I will sick and I
Will be blue.

Till the time comes
When we reunite.
How I will be sad,
To long for you, I'll fit and fight
Day after day, nite after night
They say outta mind outta
Site. For that's not true
For I could never forget
You and all that you do.
Now that your gone
I see I can cope, until

I go back to you and
Get on dope.

Then this whole poem....
Repeats and repeats. A
Dead zone my life. To stay
Or retreat.

And this aint ova, ova, ova
I say "Red rover. Send Tina
On over. To do it again,
Until she runs out."
How sad I'll be I'll pout and pout.
And then you will leave
Like you always do.
I will be sad and I will be blue.
Today I mourn,
Today I grieve.......and da saga cont.,,,,,,,

This wasn't the end of this poem; it was left unfinished. To be continued late October 2016. *Like, who knew?* This poem will have an ending that will turn this whole thing called drug addiction around. *Once an active addict, always an active addict.* Not true. Once again, God did for me what I couldn't do for myself. And by this time, I had lost count.

I didn't' know how much this next verse would mean to me in the months to come but I knew that I must be strong, brave and believe by my faith in God to know He's always with me. I had to trust Him. And that's exactly what I did.

Have I not commanded you to be strong and courageous. Do not be frightened, and do not be dismayed, for the LORD your God is with you wherever you go. Joshua 1:9 ESV
P.S.

Not knowing what lay ahead of me for the year 2016, I brought the New Year in going into one of the worse hospitals in Palm Beach County. It set the stage, beginning the scene for the rest of the year 2016. From the east coast to the west coast of Florida, I would be in four different hospitals, two nursing homes, an infusion center and a stroke rehabilitation facility before I would ever return home to what I call Fort Myers. I moved here in 2014 around Christmas time to change my life for the better. As you just read what my life consisted of: running back and forth from one side to the coast to the other, much confusion, no stability and cunning unmanageability. I was not discharged from all medical facilities until right before Thanksgiving 2016. It was then I went to Orlando to see six of my grandchildren by my two daughters. Each of them had three apiece. I couldn't believe all I went through but I was determined to write my book more than ever. I knew exactly where to start, by the grace of God. So let me tell you how I got to this point. When I realized that my life had a purpose and I was ready for an awaking of the spirit. I took this last chapter of 2016 month by month so you could understand the changes that were about to take place in my life to come.

Post-Scripture.

Chapter 20 - Year 2016
Dedicated: To the family of Rachel 'China' Bey

December 31, 2016

We called her Rae – Rae,

She was my friend.

Jose say she was my bae,bae'.

When she died' ; All of us confused

All of us mystified.; All of us cried – at one time

All of us used –

Why she gone? I question...When I hear her name mentioned...

Who did it? Way dey at? Damn detect's don't' even know da answer to that!!!...One thing we do know, And that's a fact.

She's painless, And God's got your back.

Hmmm... What can I say, my prayers paid off and were finally answered. Last night, September 12, 2019, her serial killer was captured in Wpb.

You Are Loved.

Rae, Rae – China Bey - The detects finally found 'em thru DNA

As we all pray - On earth deeply you're missed and loved

And that's a fact, Cuz, we know where you at-

-'cause Jesus got u back.

"And the sky was decorated with the perfect colors of beauty – of pinks and blues representing beautiful you. I know the angels sang you thru the gates in Heaven's place, that's a fact and - you were set free and saw God's face, we know where you at, cause God's got you back..."

The LORD is slow to get angry, but his power is great,
and he never lets the guilty go unpunished...
Nahum 1:3 NLT

Who knew that Rachel would save other lives with her death? Not only did she save mine, she solved three cold cases so far in the Daytona area where her capturer was from... (to be continued and updated in future book)

Chapt.20- Last Chance

... the Lord stood with me and gave me strength so that I might preach the Good News... And he rescued me from certain death.
2 Timothy 4:17 NLT

January 2016

After Christmas was over, I started the new year back in the hospital again with the worse pains in my stomach one could imagine. My lil' girl called 911 and the EMTs came. I was put directly into the ER and examined. Definitely there was something going on inside. I couldn't keep anything down along with diarrhea. I thought, "If I could only get a bed in detox but the hospital was the best next thing. I stayed for about a week and the pains stopped with the medication and still the doctors couldn't come up with a diagnosis. So, I took it upon myself to do things my way and I discharged myself. I pulled out the IV tube, got dressed, and had my daughter pick me up. I went AMA. Against Medical Advice. She was so mad at me. I assured her I was better and the doctors were a bunch of 'quacks.' She agreed with the latter but told me I made the wrong decision to leave. I explained to her, I could do this by myself.

All I needed was a bed in detox. From that moment on we drove to look for a detox that had a bed available. We found a detox but they didn't have a bed. I told her I needed to use, so I wouldn't be sick. She threw $40 at me in disgust and I hated myself for hurting her and the reality of what drugs has done to me and those close around me. By this time in my life, drugs/opiates especially had totally bankrupt me mentally, emotionally and physically again and again this kept happening to me and now I was at my end my bottom. I had gotten worse and *'worsa'* in a short span of time. By this time all I had left was faith in a God that I'd never seen before and I believed that He could once more work another miracle in my life like He's done before.

The am came quickly and that morning I woke up in pain. I wasn't in a hospital or a detox center. And I thought, "I'm already dope sick but it was already too late." I became too sick to even walk into a detox center by now. I couldn't even control my own bodily waste. It was coming out of both ends. I was helpless, powerless and I felt defeated again. I knew these feelings all too well. I tried to do it my way and it didn't work. All I could do was lay on my daughter's couch and I felt my life being stripped away from me. In agonizing desperation, I asked God once more to help me. "Whatever you do Lord, no matter what, just let me live to tell my story of how wonderful you have been to me.Amen"

Just after that prayer, I felt a bit of relief as I gasped for air, I told my daughter to call 911 again!!

This time I was in bad, bad shape. I had gotten at my *'worsest'* that I had ever been. My stomach had swelled. I became incontinent and vomited profusely. The same paramedics came again that had just been there a week ago. I muttered, "I don't want to go to the same hospital." They simply told me, that wasn't their problem because everyone living in this district automatically is sent there. I remembered rolling my eyes at them and when they asked me questions, I ignored them. I heard them saying in the ER that I wasn't cooperating with them and I was *'their problem now'*.

Later that night, I was ushered upstairs on the floor. My room was *comfortable and clean and for the first time, in a long time, I felt safe and secured* with the presence of God. Some things you just know and I know God was there with me, holding me. I remember thinking, I just got the best sleep in a long, long time. It was very peaceful. I guess the rest was preparing me to what was later to come. I prayed to Him that evening and I knew I couldn't do this anymore. I was tired of this vicious cycle. I confessed to Him that I no longer had a grip on my life and I am coming to believe in His power since He has brought me through many, many storms, so many, many times.

I promised God I would not leave on my own self will, especially without the advice of the medical team. So, no more AMA for me those days are gone. Remembering so many times in my past that I would pull that card this time those days were over. For the first time I meant what I said to God there would be no more unkempt promises coming out of my mouth again. I had a moment of clarity for the first time in my life. I was telling the real *truth.* I had never been so certain about believing what I promised.

Something was happening to me, I couldn't understand it at the time but it felt so right. It was God working in my heart and lifting my spirit. I believed for the first time in my body, heart and soul that Jesus took me under His wing. It says that in the Word in **Matthew 11:29 KJV Take my yoke upon you and learn of me.** From that instant the Savior became my refuge. Little did I know at that time of disparity, in my life that I was giving one of Gods most precious gifts. T'was the gift of *desperation.*

Just about 4 am in that hospital bed, I felt so comfortable but instantly, I became suddenly increasingly so cold and in such excruciating pain. They gave me my selective *medicine* and still that didn't work. I called the nurse again and told her I was going to vomit. Before she could even give me the meds to stop the feeling of pain, I turned my head to the right side of the bed, grabbed the trash can and vomited. What came was bright red blood, with blood clots as big as the palm of my hand to follow.   I saw terror come across her face as she pushed the "Rapid Response Signal."

It was just then; all the nurses came in the room and the doctor that was on duty that night. There were crash carts, oxygen devices, and contraptions I had never seen before. And yet still, I couldn't stop vomiting blood!! It was then I heard the nurse call The Blood Donor Center, that was located right in the middle of the hospital, asking to get 5 pints ready for transfusion for my blood type and to locate a bed in ICU stat. There was a pause then the doctors said, "No you better make that 8 pints of blood". After hearing all that commotion going around, I started to get really dizzy and out of breath. They put the oxygen mask on me and moved my bed and all into the elevator. The last thought that came to my mind, I better say my last prayer because I surely didn't want to die. I felt like this was my *last chance* to plead my case to God. I was finished with a life that was full of torment and torture by my own hands. So, I began to pray:

Sweet Jesus I believe that you died so I could be free. So, God I ask you for one last request. Please give me another chance at my life to serve you one more time. Please God, don't let me die like this.

And with that I shut my eyes and I didn't wake up until February 9, 2016. I wasn't sure at this time if God heard my finale and last plea for my life and give me the chance (one more time). I wouldn't know the answer to that; only by if I woke up from this horrible nightmare. At which I did. I felt a transformation starting to take place the moment I opened my eyes. I felt like the old me was gone and I was ready for the new me. It was at that moment that I turned my life and my will over to the care of God which I call Jesus. It simply states in the Word what was happening to me.

Colossians 3: 9-10 AMP Do not lie to one another, for you have stripped off the old self with its evil practices, [10] and have put on the new [spiritual] self who is being continually renewed in true knowledge in the image of Him who created the new self—

When I awoke, I had a tube down my throat, IV needles in every artery from my neck on to my thighs. I had PIC lines in both of my arms that piggyback IV tubes. My kids were on each side of the bed. My daughter later told me that they counted twenty-eight machines keeping me alive. The doctors came in and explained to me that I had a GI bleed and that they couldn't find it for the first three days and bled internally. I had to be intubated and then put on life support. The reason why my kids were all there because they had to make a decision that day to take me off this life support system or give me more time. For some reason it's like I knew they were there it's like I was watching them from above and it was just time to wake up. "Boy I had such a good sleep," I thought. Until they all told me how lucky I was and how I scared them. Then I remembered. I remembered how I was throwing up blood and all the pain and how desperate I was for God for just one more chance. I turned my life and my will over to the care of God.

I was stunned when I processed what had happened to me almost two weeks ago. I was amazed, yet perplexed. I could only summarize it like this. "I was be-*dazzled because* I just had the *beJesus* knocked into me," In other words, and in layman terms, I now literally had the fear of God in me. Pun intended. I realized how I played with my life and how I was so disloyal to God. And I thought about all the many times He saved me and brought me out of misery and despair by His grace and mercy. I believe that God saved me to make a difference in somebody else's life and tell my story of how He saved me and set me free. With my proof, from the Bible in **Proverbs 9:10 The fear of the Lord is the beginning of wisdom, and knowledge of the Holy One is understanding.**

"He that conquers himself is greater than he who conquers a city." This is what I read in one of my recovery books. For the first time, it actually made sense to me. I finally moved out of his way and stepped aside of myself. I realized I had a lot of work to do on myself and I was ready this time to do whatever it takes. That day you could say that I woke up in the third step of a 12-step recovery program. Yes, I turned my will and my life over to Him. I also realized how much God's favor had always been with me.

It wasn't long before they remove the tube out of my throat and I was able to speak. I still had a long way to go. I told my daughter to bring me my writing tablet and a pen and I began to write. I still couldn't really process this whole thing. So many nurses and student doctors came in to look at me and tell me what a miracle I was and how close I came to dying. I was the talk of the hospital for the next two weeks. I even got a chance to thank the nurse that called the rapid response the night at I was hemorrhaging. I had really scared her and she told me she helped me to recount the events that led up to that night. I was talking to her like a normal person after she had given me the medicine. She said she was surprised that I had called her back so soon to my room because I became pale and white within a matter of minutes. She said she had known something was really wrong. As I started remembering more and more and I started writing more and more. This is taken as is quoted exactly, from my actual journal.

February 23, 2016

Well where do I start? How about when I woke up that's what I seem to remember first. So when I woke and didn't know that I actually woke up from the trauma. 13 pints of blood I received they said Looking back in hindsight, what the doctor said, 'impressionable, you did good.' I can't believe I almost bled to death. And in coma for almost 9 days. They say I am moving up stairs to another floor and that I would have to share a room. As long as she was a female and not a man. Tonite it's cold. I'm not liking this hospital at all. But they did save my life. I still can't believe I almost died. Thank you, God, for my life. Now tonight they tell me this is just temporary but I'll be going to a nursing home tomorrow to continue taking antibiotics. that's not something I'm looking forward to as long as I'm alive I'll deal with it. I just think God that I'm alive.

February 24, 2016

I made it here yesterday in the middle of the night they move me I can't believe it. Great this lady here next to me is like howling and there's somebody else down the hall screaming and the place smells like piss. I know God's here with me the first thing I saw was cats big old fat cats there's two of them. Thank you, God you know, I love cats.

February 26, 2016

Well today the darn physical therapy people came in. And I know I got to go is part of the plan have to get up every day at 10 .5 days a week that really sucks cuz I hate to get up early I always have. These old folks in here be talking out their mind. I really feel sorry for them don't even get any visitors. Now just came back and they told me that my medication is coming from the pharmacy down the street like what kind of crap is that. that's why I hate coming to these nursing homes or rehabilitation centers they call it. I don't think these people really care about you it's the insurance. And you have to stay if you want to live. Seems like when I've looked around nobody seems to really go home. Most of them are in wheelchairs and just sitting in the hallways looking so sad. Like they families had forgotten about them. Okay I'm getting sleepy and waiting on my night meds. And I'm still waiting on my first dose Now by this time I've missed like 6 sets of medication and things are not looking brighter for me.

I wonder how they can get away with this not giving you your medicine. Telling her I'm starting to get freaking headaches again. They say all they can do is give me Tylenol and it helps a little bit but it doesn't take it all away. What takes away my pain is writing and praying and talking to the nurses that I will listen. I'ma try to get some rest tonight. I can't sleep it's like almost 2 o'clock in the morning. I keep on thinking how I almost died it's like I'm having PTSD. doctors coming in tomorrow so I'm going to talk to him about how I'm feeling. I tossed and turned all the way until the morning.

But my hell wasn't over; it was only beginning. See those headaches never really went away. It just got worse no matter what they did nothing helped. I ended up coming down with a high fever and the ambulance was called. It was then I was shipped like precious cargo back to the same hospital that I had just came from. It was then, the doctors called in more doctors like the specialist. Then a neurologist was called in for me along with a CAT scan. There appeared to be what seem like a mass on my left frontal lobe. Another diagnosis was determined that I had a severe case of Spondylosis. The neurologist ordered me to get fitted for a back brace by an orthopedic engineer. By what they were telling me, my conditions were serious.

I think back now, looking at my records and all the places I have been, I believe they really just didn't know what was wrong because they just couldn't figure it out that I was having my first stroke. So, they gave me several different kinds of steroids, more injections and antibiotics that I never even heard of along with plenty more tests to come.

Most of the doctors here were like very young and the set of doctors that I saw in the beginning when I had the GI bleed, I never saw any of them again. I guess they were all gone and moved on or graduated or something. I don't know I couldn't put my finger on it. This place was just weird here. It's like I never saw the same doctor twice. They will go on some kind of rotation or something. But no matter what happened to me, I just wanted to live. I almost felt like a guinea pig and they were experimenting on me. Whateva as long as I'm alive that's all that mattered to me.

March 3, 2016

I haven't written in days.   Today's my mom's birthday and my grandson. And I feel like crap. The last couple of days are really catching up with me in my mind. Let me get these words out of my head.   I'm going to write.

That's when I wrote this poem of what happened.

<u>*Death / Life Of An Addict 2*</u>

" Death of an addict,
I can't deny.
One second here,
the next I die".

Gone Too Soon,
She can't understand.
Are there hopes and dreams, not what she planned.
As she asked God, 'just one more chance'
And God blinked His eyes and with a nod and a glance.
And gave her request, nodding He granted
A new seed of life, another start within her He planted.
Now she gets better and looks deeply on her life,
Her hell finally over and most of her strife.

Later that day I called a friend and I asked him to bring me the recovery big book. He did and we went over about a doctor in the book and his opinion along with a story. It was then I realize that me and this guy named Bill had like the same experiences of the 12-steps going on in a hospital. That's when I really started taking the pen to the paper and start writing out my fourth step of a 12-step recovery program. Boy did I fill up the paper. I was stubborn hard-headed I had an inferior complex and very impatient. I was selfish and self-centered. I always thought that I could do this my way but by doing it my way it didn't get me very far.

Here I was back in the same old hospital that saved my life and they couldn't tell me what that mass was on my left frontal lobe. So, I stayed there for a little while and I was moved again to another hospital. Kindred Hospital to be exact. And this is where my hell really began. At first It was a relief to be here because there when the morning came, it's true, Joy comes in the morning. My doctors that knew from when I had my h heart surgeries were here. I knew then things were going to be alright. I was in a huge room that they used for isolation patients, that was all that was available. It was very roomy with big huge windows with curtains that looked like drapes for privacy. I had a choice here to look out it not. Walking to the bathroom was my exercise. A phone, a remote and TV shows and the best part I didn't had be to share my room with no one, there was only one nurse per 2 or 3 patients. It was like I had my own private nurse.

Come to find out that this hospital, Kindred that I was in, was for seriously ill patients that were on life support. They were held upstairs and their families didn't want them off or they were waiting for a spot in a nursing home somewhere. They seemed to be too sick for a normal hospital and too sick to go home. I was told this was a step-down type of hospital. This place was good to me though. It was here that I realized that I had a serious condition going on in my brain. I realized things didn't look good. It wasn't long after I got there, I started getting high fevers again and the most terrible headaches I have ever experienced. All the doctors could tell me was the mass on my left frontal lobe and it seemed to be getting bigger with each Cat Scan they ran. I seemed to be getting weaker and at times like when my meds came, I felt better but it never lasted long. They had given me the pain patch and changed it every 3rd day. I was medicated as needed, but something else was terribly wrong with me. I felt I was maybe having a stroke. Then my head would stop hurting and I would just sleep. I was very grateful for Kindred Hospital and on one of my better days, I managed to put my gratefulness in a poem called Kindred Spirits.

March 22, 2016

"Kindred Spirits"

I woke up in a hospital
    couldn't believe my eyes.
This place was clean, and
    in a room big size.
All the nurses are so attentive
    which made it easy to be positive.
Kindred when two souls come
    together for a good reason.
All the teamwork, pleasin -
    Very pleasn'.
How do I feel today? God let me write a poem or something.
I missed a lot of my life
    by doing the wrong thing
Not coming home; the streets,
    I'd run on a binge.
Thought I was invincible, that
    I could not die.
Thought I got this around
    My finger, but life passed
    me right by.
What the heck! Where'd everyone go,
    I'm all alone, what happen!
    I do not know.
Sitting here contemplating on

132

what to do next
Is not that hard reaching
      For the N/A text.
No longer am I perplexed.
My life today is not of my own.
Its GOD' selected at His best.

It was just a matter of time that my symptoms would be back, worsening more than ever. My high fevers were so bad that they had to pack bags of ice under my neck, inside the nook of my armpits and between my legs. Just to keep my temp at a safe level. I was freezing and my teeth were chattering and I was shivering uncontrollably. I just couldn't get warm and they surely weren't letting me. I came to despise the nurses. I really thought they were torturing me. That hurt my feelings so bad because was I really liked it here.

In this time with distress, I remembered within the last month all that happened to me and how my life used to be like. Remembering how I almost bled to death and how wonderful God has been. He gave me another chance; so, I surrendered all over again, believing that God did not bring me this far to leave me now. So, I let His will be done and not my own. And so, I put my total trust in Him and closed my eyes. When I opened my eyes, I was being transported back to that dreadful hospital that I had despised. This would be my third time this year.

I Knocked; He Answered.
Part 2

Things were fuzzy for a few days and I couldn't understand what it was that the doctors were trying to tell me. My oldest son had driven over from Fort Myers during the night since he was on my emergency contact list. He informed me that I had a stroke and that the doctors told him that there was some kind of infection stirring inside of me, but they didn't know where. This hospital was very aware of all my medical issues and health records. Without any real evidence, they assumed that the fevers were probably due to another infection in my heart. But a TEE (Trans esophageal echocardiography) must be done to confirm the diagnosis of what they think it could be. This was a test that showed pictures of my heart valves and if there were infection being able to tell by the use of a little camera. That result came back negative.

In the meantime, my white blood cell count continued to soar increasingly higher every day. This could only mean one thing there was infection is still present in the body. This time a MRI was scheduled to look into my brain at the mass. At the last minute that was cancelled due to my pacemaker was not compatible with the machine. Then another C-scan was done and that revealed some kind of abscess from my wires that connects to my pacemaker. My son was told that I would be needing surgery on my heart but my body was too weak and again, I wouldn't survive the operation.

I was in and out of consciousness throughout the days and at night. I opened my eyes to see where I was. After about a week there, my body still was not able to withstand any kind of surgery and different plans were being made. My son then came in to tell me that I had a tumor on my brain and an abscess on my heart and there wasn't much they could do but wait. Almost another week came, went by and my daughters were taking turns to be by my side. They managed to be with me and still be able to take care of their own kids too. I see now through their eyes they made it work. They had to stick together and be there for each other.

My son's now ex-girlfriend also helped out too. She would even drive over from the West coast to see about me. I know today they sit back and still talk about how sick I was and how I made it out. As for me, I give all the glory to God. It took me a long time to step aside and move out of His way and let His power work in me. I feel, "How's He going to open the door and come in, if I am standing in the way of the entrance?" This brought me to another scripture:

Matthew 7:7 KJV - Ask, and it will be given you. Seek, and you will find. Knock, and it will be opened for you.

Coming Home

One of my last entries before I lost feeling in my right side of my body from stroke number 2, which totally paralyzed me and loss of consciousness for days at a time. It's like I would be up aware of my surroundings and then lapsed into a deep, long sleep. I look back now at my journals and I see how my hand writings were so sloppy and very illegible and short. I wrote how I was feeling at that time and what my goal was for that day. I kept my goals simple and reachable.

April 1, 2016

Wow, it's the first. I just had a visit from my Nuke & JoJo. It was very pleasant. Also, we had lunch and she laid Joel next to me. I played with him and talked to my other grandson. She left and now I missed them.

Feelings - a lil better than yesterday. And that's saying a lot. I was informed today I didn't have no cardiac stuff wrong with me... Thank God.

Goal - Today my goal is to read my devotional book and do the workbook. My lil girl's birthday is tomorrow.

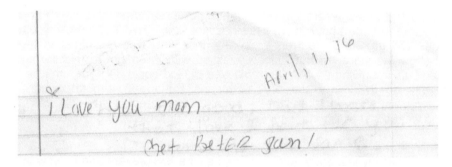

Awwwh...I just read what she wrote in my book. This is so sweet of her. I have to get better for my beloved.

Dear God,
Thank you for everything, my health, the good & the bad. Please don't let me die, for I am not readi.

April 2, 2016

Today is my baby girl's B-day. Oh, how I remember it so vividly, she was my Easter Baby. So perfect she is. Well now she's got her own kids and I love them so. My girls are very close at heart, for that I am truly grateful. I wish my sister & I was close. But I messed that up a long time ago. How I wish I could take it back.

Thru the good, bad times
That love I have for you
remains the same.
My love for you runs

deep and pure
Till…
That day I didn't
Wake
Pray

April 3, 2016
I've ran 2 fevers and I feel weak. I cried a lot today, but I'm good now. I'm in the spirit. and I'm good with that. I think about Rae Rae a lot and I have so many questions. My heart hurts for her. Please God help the detec's figure it out. I'm sitting in the sunlite, baskin'.
    <u>Feelings</u> - melancholy
    <u>Goals</u> - not to get another fever and call my family.

Oh, I love you Lord. Please let me get better and take this infection from me. I beg of You, Sweet Lord. The pain gets to much for me to bear, please God how I need Your. Help. Lord I love You, and I do Your will, not my own, so God show me what it is that I should do, teach me for I'm teachable. Keep the pain away, remove it at once. Amen

During this time in the hospital I was getting tired of breathing, it became so difficult. My body became exhausted and I started to become increasingly fatigued and this is where the real fight began. I really mean litteraly I began to tussle and wrestle about in my little hospital bed. I had begun to cry out with moans and groans of surrender for my dear life I was not about to give up. Somehow the story of how Jacob wrestled with the angel for his life and like Jacob I wasn't giving up *until I am blessed.* If God could do it for him , he could certainly do it for me too. By all means I made it through once again. However,with another unseen sroke that didn't get detected yet until I was moved to the west coast of Florida; I never wrote again until October 7, 2016.

After my last entry, April the 3rd, I said a few prayers and I just wanted to leave - But I remembered I promised God I would never go AMA again without medical advice. Of course, we already know God works in the most mysterious ways. And with that, I stayed until the doctors informed my son that there once again, there was nothing they can do. My body didn't reach safe numbers for surgery and that hospice was the best advice they can give him. They convinced him I had less than thirty days to live and tomorrow the caseworker for hospice would bring the papers for him to sign.

Well I did understand that much somehow. The nurse that was taking care of me came had explained to my son that she didn't think the doctors were right and advised him to get a second opinion. So that night, I remember my oldest son coming to me and telling me what they want to do with me and he asked me to try to fight this and get better. I shook my head yes and blinked my eyes as best I could and relayed a message to him that I did want to fight this. He and the nurse also explained to me that they were moving me in the morning to hospice. I remember shaking my head, "No," and began trying to pull out the

136

catheter and IVs but I was too weak. I remember the nurse saying, "Miss Lopez, do you understand me?" I blinked my eyes and responded. She asked me, "Do you want to leave?" I blinked twice and responded. Before she asked me another question, she said, "I think you should go with your son back home!" I had her permission and she was medically advising me to leave. So, I wasn't going against medical advice. Last time I checked; nurses are part of the medical team. In my opinion, they play one of the most important part in the hospital. They work right beside the patients. And they get to see what the doctors don't see.

Tears came to my eyes, as she began to remove the catheter and IVs. It was about a shift change around midnight. It was raining. I remember being helped into the wheelchair, going down a back elevator. Then I remember my son and her putting me into the back of his car. And the last thing I remember was being so happy and the nurse crying tears of happiness as she hugged my son and assured him, he was doing the right thing. She then turned back at me and said, "God bless you Miss Lopez." We were off to Fort Myers.

I later learned that this was the same nurse I had back in February when I had the GI bleed. Although we were going to the west coast of Florida and to Lee County for a second opinion with different doctors, it seemed hopeful that we were doing the right thing (but I was not out of the woods yet) however things were about to get a little more complicated. I know you're probably thinking, *What else could go wrong?* More health issues were about to be revealed with a group of professional doctors. God really did have the last say on this one. ***The grass withereth, the flower fadeth: but the word of our God shall stand for ever. Isaiah 40:8 KJV***

Since I had already come to believe that God could save me, like I've repeated in this book of His Word of truth, God never changes. He's kept His word to me in His WORD. Somehow I knew that He will remain with me like He always has and always says He will. ***Hebrews 13:8 NASB Jesus Christ is the same yesterday and today and forever.***

May 2016
___

Raining, Showering & I Was Bloomingly Flowering

During this drive, I remember using the bathroom all over myself. I had no control over my bodily functions, again! I remember talking to my baby boy in Colorado. And I also remember how he flew all the way to the east coast of Florida with his girlfriend and my granddaughter, using his income tax just to come see me. And I remember that all so clearly because I got to hold little 'Leah on my lap.

He said, "Mommy, this is your son. This is your baby boy. You gotta get better Mom. You gotta do this. It's gonna be alright. I love you and I'ma come see you again." And that's all I remember. And that was the last time I was coherent. But I remember it made sense. I remember getting back to Fort Myers. I remember my oldest son and his ex-girlfriend bathing me, feeding me with a spoon; And I remember we ate Chinese food. And the next thing I knew, I'm hauled off in an ambulance on the west coast in Lee County, Florida. Because my son didn't want to tell the new doctors that we fled the east coast and what the doctors said there about putting me in hospice, it was in my best interest, just not to say anything and see what they come up with and take a second look at what's really wrong with me. And boy did my son do the right thing.

Just when things couldn't get any worse, I suffered a Grand Mal Seizure for over an hour and went into convulsions that lasted for almost twelve hours, all through the night and most of the next day. Since that seizure lasted so long, they told my son that I would have definitely permanent neurological damage. And again, I was put on life support because I could barely breathe on my own. My breaths were very shallow. And I remember I was praying in between breaths. I was very weak and it seemed like it took too much energy to take a breath. I had to hang on because I knew that this would eventually pass. That same voice, that I had heard before said, *"It will only be an hour. And this will pass soon. Whatever you do, don't cross the street."* It was God's voice again. And I was confident and obedient about that. I believed at that time; Jesus was taking turns with me to breath. It was like He was breathing His life into me. I believe I was walking through the shadows of my own death which brings me to the Bible verse **Psalms 23:4 ESV Even though I walk through the valley of the shadow of death I will fear no evil for thou are with me.**

The EEG was done on my brain and they had left the glue in my hair, so all my hair was glued together and it had to be cut short and because of that, I threw a fit. I never liked anybody touching my hair or cutting it. And my girls knew this. My daughters came to the west coast to help get the glue out of my hair and to see me. My girls consoled me and told me my hair was still long and just above my bra strap. To me that was short. I was so used to it touching the tip of my buttocks. So my oldest daughter braided my hair in two French braids and that day I felt more like myself. They were a blessing to have to see me through this tough obstacle of losing my hair. Looking back now, I think I really treasured my hair. Who knew in a couple more months, all my hair would fall out? God was preparing me I think. To take it all at one time would be too drastic for me at that moment in my life.

They also made sure that the nurses were taking care of me properly. Since both of my daughters were in the medical field, they seemed to the only ones I could trust. I remember telling my daughter I wanted some smoke neck bones and collard greens. She assured me that she would make me some when I get better and come home. And she kept her promise. I was not realizing at the time I was being showered with blessings of getting better a little bit at a time. One distinct memory that resurfaced was the verse John 3:16. I was trying to say it out loud but I couldn't hear myself talk. The nurses kept telling my son, "your mom keeps making funny sounds and muttering something but I can't understand what she is saying." I knew what I was saying and hat I was believing in my heart. Its what I never forgot that carried with me and through all these years.

June 2016

I was starting to get my senses back. I couldn't see. I didn't even know when I had to urinate or have a bowel movement. They ended up putting an adult diaper on me. I couldn't push the call bell, the nurses checked on me in a somewhat timely manner. I just couldn't eat anything because I didn't know how to swallow. So, a feeding tube was then inserted in my belly button. And that's how I received nutrition, a liquid diet. (Mmm... yum yum. Just what I always wanted.) I ended up staying here in the hospital until the middle of June. I was discharged out of the stroke unit and left in a wheelchair and was provided home healthcare. I had to have a nurse twenty-four hours a day at home. My son and his girlfriend at the time split the nighttime shift. I wasn't home no more than twelve days and came down with another fever.

So, my son called the ambulance and the EMTs said I had a high fever and given my history, I needed immediate attention. Blood tests were administered and my white blood count was high, which indicated infection. Where? They didn't know. So I underwent more tests. The next morning, they came to the conclusion that I had a UTI infection. And there was more terrible news. I was antibiotic unfriendly. So, I would have to be given chemotherapy infusion for three weeks, thirty minutes a day. I was told there would be some minor side effects... like losing my hair and going bald. And boy did I lose my hair. ***Why, every hair on your head has been counted! Don't be afraid, you are worth more than many sparrows. Luke 12:7 CJB*** But I remember making a promise to God, back on the east coast. Since I always thought my hair was my crown, I remembered sayin', "God, I don't care if I go bald headed and you take all my hair, just let me live to do your work." Not only did He restore my hair eventually but it came back full, wavy and thick. What the heck?!! Not be bragging about myself but it's beautiful! I never had hair like this before. And that's all I got to say about that.

Until this day, I believe God came back and collected on a promise I made and I was fine with that cause He always kept His promises to me. When I look back it reminds of me of the verse in Joshua. I remember it so well because that's my first grandchild's name. **Joshua 23:14 ESV "...All of you, that not one word has failed of all the good things that the Lord your God promised concerning you. All have come to pass for you; not one of them has failed."**

July 2016

Oh, and one more thing, I had to learn to do everything over again, like a baby learning how to walk, crawl and feed themselves. I would have to go into a physical/occupational rehabilitation center also known as O.T. and P.T. I would have to learn how to walk and dress myself all over again. I would also have to learn to cook, fold laundry and use my hands to pick up pegs. I couldn't pick up stuff. I also didn't have any fine motor skills at all. Also, I wouldn't be home again until the end of July, if the doctors saw fit to release me. As it turned out, I was released at the beginning of August. This month I would be fifty years old. What an awesome gift, to go home. I was released of my obsession to use drugs. I could finally say to myself. *"I was done and I ain't never gonna relapse again."* And to this day, I never have. This is how the rest of 2016 goes down and I'm taking this month by month. Because it seemed like every month, something different was happening to me. I kept turning it over to God because I knew this battle was not mine, it is the Lord's; For this is even written in the Bible: **1 Samuel 17:47 KJV: And all this assembly shall know that the Lord saveth not with sword and spear: for the battle is the Lord's, and he will give you into our hands.**

August 2016

50 Plus One

Somehow it never ceases to amaze me how God works. This month turning fifty years old, I also remembered that I used to tell God all the time, I was only partying until I was fifty. And boy, He made sure I kept that promise. I say once again, *"God does for us, what we can't do for ourselves."* Even though my sight was failing due to age and the three strokes, it became clear to see my life in reality for the first time. For my birthday that year, I received my first pair of glasses. Lucky me. I was actually delighted. My son took me out to a Japanese Restaurant with a hibachi grill and I couldn't have been happier to see myself live to turn fifty years old. Even though I still walked with a walker long distance, for my birthday, the walker was put up and I broke the cane out. I told my son I would be needing his assistance cause I would be walking very little with my cane tonight. It was like starting all over again from scratch. From learning how to swallow my food, learning how to walk, knowing when the urge to go to the

140

bathroom felt like and figuring out how comprehend the simplest tasks. It was sort of like being a toddler all over again. I remember in the Bible coming to God as *little child.* **Matthew 18:3 NLT Then he said, "the I tell you truth, unless you turn from your sins and become like little children...**

September 2016

Taking Baby Steps

I understood this verse by what God was transforming me to be, a new creation. By the time September rolled around, I was attending outside P.T. three times a week and I was getting better and better. The days rolled by, on and on, but I felt like something was missing. I prayed to God, something was bothering me, yet I couldn't understand. Then it came to me, I needed to write. I needed to get out what I was feeling. September turned into October and on 10/07/16, I would journal for the first time. Well, at least I tried to. I would practice the alphabet, uppercase and lowercase. I did the best I could. I had to recollect how writing took the anxiety out of me and let me see the truth of how I was feeling. I really had to lean on God. I became totally reliant on Him. I was determined to write. I wasn't going to let nothing get in my way. I will rise up like the eagle. A bald eagle to be exact literally. My hair had fallen out but I kept the scarf on so no one could see it. I had never lost my hair before. But I remember that promise I made to God while still on the east coast. After all my oldest child, my son, would say, "Ma it's just hair. It'll grow back. Would you just relax and calm down?" *"And I would sternly reply,"* Fredrick! Shut up! It's not just hair to me!" In **Matthew 10:30 (NIV) "And even the very hairs of your head are all numbered."** God knows how many I had and how many I lost. It is funny, when my hair grew back, it came in curly and fine like a child's hair.

READER'S ALERT

All the poems and journals you just read from 2003 up until this point are all B.S. No silly not the cuss words, it stands for before stroke (B.S.). And everything you will read from this moment on, all poems and journals, are A.S.S. the Aftershock Stroke stories. The first writings are written after I learned to write again. Everything that you've read are from actual journals from jails to hospitals to institutions. They were typed exactly how I wrote them, wrong, misspelled and all. It's only by God's grace that I was able to find a blessed friends that stuck with me through thick and thin of the entire writing of this book.

Progress Not Perfection
Part 1

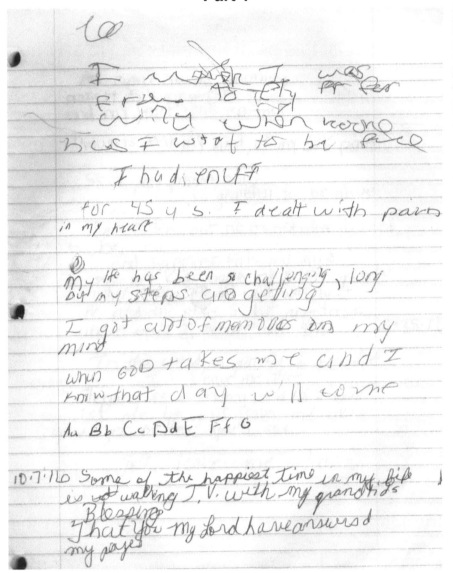

10-11-16
    I haven't written for a long time and it's time for a change. In my heart, I miss my kids and I can't read my own writing. I stop and wonder why it is God didn't tell me what to to do. Does he want me to take care of Joel? I always

wanted him. Due to circumstances, I'm trying to write good. I'm trying to write good and my girls are here. God please bless over my grandkids.

10-12-16

As red as the blood of Jesus is, is my love for you. I promise to love you with all God can give me. I love you Joel and God has your back. I will never give up on you. You are one of many miracles of our Lord. As my grandson, I cannot watch you go on, without the things you need to be like the rest of your cousins. Just hold on, Grandma's coming to see you at the beginning of November. I love you. You are loved.

Love,
Grandma

10-15-16
Listening to Johnny Cash and thinking about yest. My girl is so slick in more ways than one. I need to do more soul searching, pray, share and put it all together of what happened. Draw my conclusions, and let it go. Seriously God. I pray for your understanding and knowledge.

> *God <u>grant</u> me the <u>serenity.</u>*
> *To <u>accept</u> the things I cannot change,*
> *The <u>courage</u> to change the things I can,*
> *And the <u>wisdom</u> to know the difference.   -Reinhold Niebuhr*

Grant - give
Serenity- calmness/the peace
Accept - receive
Courage- braveness - brave
Wisdom - intellect

As I look back now, every time there's a problem, I would remember the Serenity Prayer and dissect it. It wasn't until I started going to Grace Church in the central location that I found out there was more to the Serenity Prayer. And that's what I needed. I needed to hear about Jesus. Just the name itself has so much power. It was then that I started dissecting the second half of the Serenity Prayer which

goes like this::
Living one day at a time,
enjoying one moment at a time;
accepting hardship as a pathway to peace;
taking, as Jesus did,
this sinful world as it is,
not as I would have it;
trusting that You will make all things right
if I surrender to Your will;
so that I may be reasonable happy in this life
and supremely happy with You forever in the next.
Amen.

Reinhold Niebuhr

As awake in the morning
anxiety fills my chest
and my heart beats so fast

Thoughts fill my mind, of my dark past

So I pray, THANK GOD,
so grateful to be alive.

HAIR fallen out, no its not what it used
to be,
and happiness fills my mind.
To see my kids again my beloved grands
when I thought all hope was lost
He paid the price on that rugged cross
where would I be without Him.   10·25·16

In this world, so grateful to be alive.
Just leave me alone
Sleeping so soundly, and they wont
let me be, just leavn me alone
+ get better you'll see

When I tell you I had a case of the P's I ain't lying! I would practice and pray with my pen and paper. Proceeded by praising all the while repenting for all the wrong I've done to myself and others by not sticking to my promises to God. I needed God's power in me for I realized now I had a purpose and a position in this life. For within myself I became pleasingly pleased and at peace that truly surpassed all of my carnal understanding. I knew then Jesus heard my pleas just as it states in the Word. **Philippians 4:7 And the peace of God that surpasses all understanding will guard your hearts, in Jesus Christ.**

Today I feel I must lead by being an example of how Gods grace and his love for me has alwys saved me. **Titus 2:3-4 NKJV Tell the older women… they are to teach what is good, so that they might encourage the young…**

God - Simple as a Cat

GOD IS LOVE
And for certain
I know its true:

First He showed me,
something so simple
as simple as a orange cat.

Then HE showed me tru
a frut; the orange
so juicy
something so sweet tasting

I was convinced and that's
thought of fact.

He has brought thru
life and death many, many
times
I cant even begin to
count.
what prayer, after prayer
HE answered them
without HE didnt have a
DOUBT

In Memory of A Beloved Cat: Luna Perez (8/1/2000-12/8/18)
Luna the beloved pet is still loved and deeply missed to the moon and back. For eighteen carnal years she lived on this Earth not like the cat years in Heaven be.

I look back at all my cats that I loved lost and I felt the pain of losing a pet. So I said a silent prayer to myself and dedicated this poem to Luna and all my cats that went before her. To anyone that's lost a pet for we all know they become a member of our family. I believe that's what pets are for, love and patience. That's how I came to write Simple As A Cat. In WV I had a orange tabby cat. I discovered that God is love. It was so simple. While eating an orange it was so sweet and juicy. It was then my cat rubbed against my ankles that's when the notion hit me. 'God is real'. For how can someone make the color orange,a orange fruit and a cat with stripes the same color that just wanted to be loved? **1 John 4:8 He that loveth not knoweth not God; for God is love.**

Simple As A Cat

"Love is God
God is love
And for certain -
I know it's true."

First, He showed me something simple,
As simple as an orange cat.
Then He showed me thru a fruit
The orange, so juicy and sweet tasting,
I was convinced and that's a fact.

He has brought me from life to death
So many many times,
I can't even begin to count.
Prayer after prayer, He's answered
Without a doubt.
From...
"Layin in the H. bed."
Beggin' for tomorrow
With smell of my death
And the sirens of sorrow.

Soon my son came to see me
With tears in his eyes,
Sobbing and beggin' "Ma please don't die."
What's a mother to do?
Holding him tight,
As I whispered in his ear, "It's gonna be alright."
Remembering those words he spoke,
"You gotta fight, Ma fight, you gotta fight."

And with those words I made it thru the night,
And many more after that.
Remembering God's love
Is as simple, as simple as an
orange cat.
                    By N. Lopez

Saying Goodbye
Part 2

Right after I had written *Simple As A Cat*, something else was being left unsaid. Something needed to get out. I scrambled looking for my black writing tablet where I wrote my *Goodbye Letter To Drugs*. Then I figured it out. It was unfinished. I needed to have an ending and I knew exactly what needed to be said so I could get closure. And I picked up right where the poem ended and I wrote my *Goodbye Letter To Drugs Part 2, The Sequel*.

Goodbye Letter To Drugs Part 2, The Sequel

Continued…
And so, the story goes on and on…
Today I mourn, Today I grieve.
Now that you're gone,
I feel deceived.
But not anymore,
Cause this has to stop.
As I speak my peace,
I will no longer be your live junkie prop.
But just before you leave,
I want you to know,
You gotta leave,
You gotta roll.
So hit the road Jack,
And don't look back,
Cuz I won't be here no more.
But just a few more words before we part,
Not only did you literally break my heart,
I'm sick and tired of being your fool.
I'm sick and tired of feeling blue.
I'm sick and tired of doing all those crazy things that I did for you.
Waking up, feeling dope sick-
Crying… swearing it would be different this time,
But I knew you was lyin'.
I was so sick in a matter of seconds,
You gave me instant gratification,
Oh, how you made me feel brand new,
Not really knowin' I played the fool.
A mechanical heart valve,

And a pacemaker,
I was always the giver,
And you was always the taker.
And if that's not enough,
I knew I was always so broke.
Instead of being satisfied with my money,
You turned around and gave me a GI Bleed and 3 strokes.
And for real,
That wasn't all.
You gave me a Grand Mal Seizure,
At my expense, And your leisure.
And again, you left and I was deceived,
And this time I didn't grieve.
Laying in the hospital bed,
God spoke to me and said,
After I begged,
"Just one more chance,
Just one more song,
Just one more dance,
This has been coming for so long.
To do things right.
To spread my story,
With Your word's Lord,
Your Honor,
Your Glory.
And God heard my cries,
As I say to you,
"Good riddance,
Goodbye..."
So with a nod he granted,
Another seed he planted,
So I can be
Clean, serene,
And set free.

Joel 2:25 God can fix and restore what is broken; Just believe in Him and have faith.

I had an appointment with my neurologist for an updated C-Scan to see how much damage the three strokes had done. I was feeling really dizzy and lightheaded. My neurologist said, *"It's probably because of the two different kind of seizure medications."* Taking action, he discontinued the Dilantin and gave me a blood test. I had found out I reached dangerous toxic levels. Even though I stopped the medication still I seemed to be getting worse by the day. On the 25th of this month, I just so happen to leave my P.T. and I was feeling really dizzy again. I went straight to the emergency room and was admitted. I had to spend the night and it just so happened to be Halloween. Trick-or-Treat. I guess I got tricked.

Apparently, there had been a mix up in communication on which seizure medication to discontinue. That mix up almost caused me my progress on my health. After spending thirty-six hours there, we finally got it cleared up. I was released on November 2nd. And I gradually got better. Once again, God had saw me through. His mercy was certainly on a continuous journey with me, still.

October – Continues

Doing Something Different
Part 3

After I wrote this as the conclusion of my past drug addiction, I felt like I had grown. I felt like I could do anything. I just didn't know where I was gonna start at. I had watched The Steve Harvey Show; I loved watching Family Feud; I love all the words. I heard him talking about a challenge he had coming up, starting on December 1st. But you must register by November 15th. So, I kept that on my mind. And I prayed about it. That was the hope I needed to hear. He talked about staying tuned in and more would be revealed because I did and more was. But first, I had to take care of my health and prioritize what was more important. That would be keeping the maintenance up on myself, starting with the first thing my drug addiction. I told myself I would find a meeting so I did just that. Meanwhile, I stayed *prayed up*. I prayed all the time. I wrote my prayers out and I started listening to Gospel and Christian music. I felt changes within myself, something was happening. I couldn't believe it. *I was really done with the life of my past.* It was time to move on and do something different. To rap this all up, it was time to let the healing begin. Because I was tired of losing so much, it was now time to win. So I got on the winning team and began to follow the Lord and my dreams.

There Is Hope

Getting out that day in the hospital, I had another doctor's appointment for my second mammogram. I call having to get a mammogram, going to see my *"Mammy."* And when I go see the OBGYN doctor, I call that, getting to see my *"Pappy."* I got good news. I didn't have to go back anymore. They had 'squoze' my breasts in that machine and I caught flashbacks of 2002. Boy, I had to hurry up and get the heck out of there. I called my daughter up in Orlando. She calmed me down and told me, *"Ma, just come here."* She didn't have to convince me no longer. I had enough of hospitals.

I talked to her about Steve Harvey having a challenge and doing the online interview and asked if she could she help me. With Thanksgiving rollin' around, and me wanting to be with my grandchildren, all 6 of them, especially Joel because he grew differently than the others. All the other grandchildren reached their milestones around the right time but Joel never did. Because of that, he grew closer to my heart; He seemed to always be looking through me. I nicknamed him my *baby Jesus.* All his cousins and siblings to this day, sing songs about him and say he was *"The best baby and cousin."* They even made up a song called, *"My Heart Beats For You."*

It's now early November and I don't know how to go about writing my book. So, I got on my one knee as best as I could, held onto the bed, and prayed. I asked God to give me answers. I waited patiently, to the best of my ability. Since I will be spending Thanksgiving in Orlando with my grandchildren, I pray that God help me some way to get started. For I had work to do and a promise to keep. It was then I waltzed into the living room, swaying back and forth on my walker. My knees and legs were hurt and stiff from bending down. And whata you know low and behold, what was coming on the television? Steve Harvey's Family Feud. It was about him having the *Jump Challenge* and the deadline was November 15.

My son's ex-girlfriend drove me up to Orlando. I stayed for Thanksgiving and played with my grandkids. I did the online interview and was accepted. It took me four hours to do. I didn't know too much about going online and from my strokes my right hand shakes and is still numb to this day. So, it's hard for me to push buttons. I didn't even really know about voice recording. The challenge was starting on the December 1st through the 21st. It was a bunch of questions about what we wanted to do in our lives but never did. It was about having regrets you live with. With this challenge, you could accomplish any dreams and it was never too late. I was excited. I prayed that I would get selected. Two hours later, I was notified by email. I wasn't the only one who wanted to write a book. I was put into a category of tens of thousands of other people that wanted to write a book. And that's how I started writing my book.

Furthermore, while in Orlando, we danced and played...all the grandkids and me. We ate. We had a really good time. I would sing and dance; We all took turns holding JoJo's hands and playing with him from his chair. He smiled a lot and made the cutest baby noises. We both would do my exercises every day. I would exercise with him and he would just laugh. All the grandkids loved to sleep with me, all six of them. We'd make a big palette on the floor in the living room and we all piled up at bedtime. They would all argue whose turn it was to sleep with me. By morning time, they would all go in separate sleeping quarters, except Joel. He would love to cuddle in the nook of my arm.

Going back, I tell you, the way my grandson would look at me sometimes, it was as if he knew something I didn't. I was getting better and I feared, maybe he thought, *"What about me?"* I felt I had to do something. So, I went running back to Jesus. I needed answers and I needed them now. *What was I gonna do? What could I do?* Waiting on answers my mind boggled. I talked to my daughter and asked her to let me take Joel back to Fort Myers to see my therapist that had a specialization in pediatrics, physical and speech therapy. My daughter needed to give me Power of Attorney for medical purposes only. I told her to think about it and I will return at Christmas to pick him up. She just nodded her head as if to say *ok.* I just wanted my grandson to get better and catch up with the other grandkids.

Soon it was time to leave and get back to Fort Myers. I kissed all my grandkids and we all cried just as my grandma did a long time ago. I assured them all that I would return by Christmas. Like who knew by the New Year, all of our lives would be changed forever? For all of our hearts would be broken, shocked and devastated. **Lamentations 3:25 NIV The LORD is good to those whose hope is in him, to the one who seeks him;** And that's what I did. I sought Him out, every single waking moment of my life because He was all the hope I had left to go on. He was the only *truth* and *promise* that I could rely and depend on. There were times to come that I felt very weary and depressed and I had to remember the verse: **Isaiah 40:29 (NIV) "He gives strength to the weary and increases the power of the weak."** I remember this emotion vividly when I was having my strokes.

"When the student is ready, the teacher will appear." Buddha Shakyamuni

I returned back to Fort Myers. December 1st came and The Steve Harvey Jump Challenge started. It was time to write my book and I knew just how to get started. A thirty-year dream is finally coming true. And at least at this time, I had an inclination on how to do it. The rest was up to God. I had to do the footwork now. So, the Jump Challenge came in handy. Nothing could stop me now. My grandson became my motivation. I had this all figured out. This was what God wanted me to do. Write, sell books, hire a specialist. And Joel would be well. Since he was born, he had been tested for his skills and functions. The doctors said he was *developmentally delayed*. We were told he would grow out of it. So, we all believed the doctors. We needed a second opinion and when we moved from the east coast to the west coast, we got that. And the doctors said the same thing. *He would grow out of it.* I thought, *"These doctors don't know what the hell they're talking about!"* And when my daughter moved to Orlando, Central Florida, she was told the same thing. We never questioned it again. We all just waited for God to do His work. And I kept it *movin'* with the book. I *journaled* and stayed accountable with the other "Jumpers."

12-01-16
I was so excited yesterday. I journaled too. I was busy praying and grateful for this day and yesterday. Day 1 - I was so nervous and texted my people in West Virginia and West Palm Beach, my old stomping grounds and announced what I was doing. I was so proud I took action about being in the challenge.

12-02-16
My priorities: 1) God first. 2) My personal responsibilities 3) Took my meds. *Even brought Coumadin to the library. 4) Revised Born a Maid since* 2004
5) Must work on my life story now.
Making so many mistakes on the phone. Can't remember how to do this. My brain is not thinking. I'm learning how to take the bus. Today has been hectic.

12-11-16
Decisions:
1. Filled out an entry form from contest today.
2. Researched Renaissance Academy.
3. Talked to my daughters.
4. Still trying to get my thoughts together.
5. Can't wait to get back to Orlando.
6. Not arguing anymore.

12-12-16

Today is about procrastination. I sewed a button on my pants, sewed a pillow for my grandkids, posted a picture, talked with my daughters, and took my meds.

Gratitude List:
1. I am grateful for physical therapy
2. Signed off today with one of my therapist & I'm discharged.
3. Grateful for my baby girl. Sent me a picture of Joel and I am grateful. I can't wait to go back for Christmas.
4. I actually sewed a button on my pillow. I can't believe it. I have so much confidence today.
5. The library and all the people that are helping me. I figured out who my heroes are.
6. Grateful for all my friends in West Virginia.
7. Cholesterol is down 100 points.
8. Hot chocolate in the library.
9. Talking to my grandkids on the phone
10. Found out my brother is in in the Philippines and he stopped drinking.
11. Today I have a plan.
12. Tomorrow looks good.

It was December 15th, a day of kindness. I remember this well because that was the day people didn't get their email for the challenge. I texted other "Jumpers," and asked if they got theirs. They were waiting also. While sitting on the edge of my bed, looking out the open window, a breeze blew in. The tree branches swayed, the leaves stirred on the trees and ground below. It was like all the dry leaves were racing and were swirling in a circle. I was just grateful I could witness that. Praying and being still, I listened for the wind and the sound of the leaves rustling. And just as surely as you're reading this, I heard a voice spoken clearly, *"It is already written."* I know who that voice was. There was no doubt and no mistaken it. The voice of God. I immediately responded, *"Where Lord? Where?"* I frantically gazed about the room. And high and behold, there it was. Old Forrest, sitting upon a hamper, opened up...was my blue, old suitcase. The same kind Forrest Gump had in the movie, except mine was another color.

There inside the suitcase was all my writings I have ever done, dating back from 2003. So, I put them in order by the dates of when they were written. I had this big wonderful plan, Joel being my motivation. I was determined to get started. See, my plan was fool proof. I was going to write this book. I was going to sell many copies. Then I was going to hire a specialist so we could figure out what the heck was really wrong with my grandson. We knew he was smart because he had all forty-six chromosomes the day, we took him home. Well, that's not exactly the way it worked out. God had much better plans than I did. I still had this weird feeling that something terrible was going to happen but I thought it was going to be me. I thought *maybe I'm going to get sick again.* So, I made sure to hold him close to me at night. *I told him that he was loved and that he was treasured by Jesus.* In a couple more days after Christmas and before New Year's, I would be going back to Fort Myers. But in the back of my mind, I still had this terrible thought. So, I made every moment and every minute and every second count.

12-29-16

Got rest. Didn't journal yesterday. Spent my last full day with the grands. Made stuffed cabbage with the girls. I grow increasingly in deep thought with my lil girl about Joel. I slept with Joel and Doo on the couch. Didn't get much sleep. Gotta get up at 4 a.m. to the Greyhound station by 5 a.m. Bus departs at 5:20.

12-30-16

Catching the bus in a few minutes. Met a very nice lady in the presence of God once again. We ate good last night and getting ready for the new year. Organizing.

When I left Orlando, my daughter refused to sign custody over to me. She wanted to take care of her son, Joel, her own self and changed her mind at last minute. I prayed the whole time in Orlando that God's will be done. I thought this was why God was getting me better, so I could take care of my grandson. And since my daughter was so young and already had another baby by this time, I thought this was what I was supposed to do. I had always had Joel with me. Sometimes I thought he was my son and not my grandson. *Who knew this would be the last time I would ever hold my grandson?* That's when I remembered one of my favorite verses:

Isaiah 55:8-9 (NKJV)

"For My thoughts are not your thoughts, Nor are your ways My ways," says the Lord. "For as the heavens are higher than the earth, So are My ways higher than your ways, And My thoughts than your thoughts.

My heart was broken because I expected to have my grandson traveling back in my arms for this New Year. And yet I was alone, all by myself. But I respected my daughter's wishes and understood why she wanted to keep him with her. But I accepted this was all God's Will. And I assured them all I would see them again soon because Christmas was right around the corner.

Chapt. 21 – Great Grief

Dedicated to Corinne, Pastor Cindy, and to everyone else in Grieve Share or anyone that has lost a child or someone dear to you.

12-31-16

New Year's Eve. I'm home. I fixed my meds, took them, prayed and went on Facebook. I called Nettie and am journaling. I am doing the challenge again for the next twenty-one days starting tomorrow. Again, what's different?

1.) New Year 2017
2) Take better notes
3) Must stay connected
4) WRITE, WRITE, WRITE

Calendar mark dates today, check doctor's appointments. Monday meetings, figure out a way to get there.

Things I'm gonna do every day:
1. Give it to God
2. Reflect
3. Connect
4. Respect

01-01-17

A rough day. A day to forget about last year's struggles and start fresh. A disturbing phone call that I wish I never got.

It was no sooner back to Fort Myers, that I received that call that my grandson Joel was on life support for his life. Total devastation; I was just down and 'dumbfoundedly' floored. *I just left there,* I thought. It was just then the words of that song came back into my mind that they sang at lil T's funeral by her Aunt Freda, *I Didn't Bring You This Far To Leave You Now.* I didn't know until I started writing this book how much more important those words of that song impacted my life. It gave me the strength not to give up and keep striving to reach my goal by remembering that verse in the bible. ***Philippians 1:6***

01-02-17

There's no one answering the phones, my text, don't know what to do. So, I give it to God. Pack a bag and plan my journey into a defaulted situation, in a defaulted Palm Beach County.

I'm frustrated, in questioning, turning to the Lord every second, so infuriated. We get there to St. Mary's Hospital. My daughter's nowhere to be seen?! Where she at? What she doing? Nurse is nasty. And I'm ready to give them the "what for." My lil girl came. She's a mess. I can't leave her. Must get her to safety. Got to take the boys with me.

I see Joel. Tubes everywhere. PIC lines, monitors, IV's, open glass viewing, and one nurse per room. I rub my hands across his forehead into his hair and I swear I saw his eyelids flutter for a half second. Could that be a response? I sayeth my peace, with him and I'm OK. Only because Joel is peaceful. His spirit has already gone to the Lord. "The Lord giveth and the Lord taketh away."

Home with boys. My ex has to come thru. Cause now is not the time for getting mad and holding resentments. He's mad at my lil girl.

He did come to her. He put on his cowboy hat, boots with the spurs and 'Cow Boyed up.'

Thank God.

My oldest daughter showed up in almost an overlap. My lil girl sleeps. Joel is peaceful. So now my turn. We all made it home. The boys and I, and we are in for the night.

01-03-17

I'm up as I wait on the word from the hospital. God's timing. I'm not in doubt anymore. For the good shall come out of this situation and more will be revealed in God's time, not mine. Must be patient for God will never leave you. I must be open and awake, alert and answers will come. God has his own definition of His own words. After all, He who has already written the dictionary of life. He has installed in many men. Amen.

The boys slept.

Goal: is to write my goal out and stick to it. I will write my story page by page, bit by bit, to get the book finished and seek the Lord for Q / A.

Feelings: I feel motivated, ambitious, curious, and concerned.

Goal: Get thru today and with a sigh of relief, as I "Let go and let God."

My oldest daughter just called and said, "Ma it's over. They baptized him, took his footprints, and fingerprints and hair clippings. They call that memories."

Just to sum everything else up together, I was hit dead center with a dagger and never even saw that one coming. I thought everything would go back to *normal* but I didn't know what normal was because I had been on this rollercoaster for so long. One thing I did know I couldn't give up on my dream of writing a book. Joel became my motivation now more than ever and I was determined to get this done. Nothing was gonna stop me. No fire, no friends, nor family or death would interfere with my goal of writing my book. And on the flip side, I was ghastly grief stricken. I believed it was the element of surprise that really got me.

01-04-17

I got discombobulated and anxiety. And I'm in a bad mood. I'm gonna tell my son today how much I appreciate him. And his girlfriend too. My goal is to find my pens and stay out of my old memories of what could have been. Think about the good times and stay in the now and not in the 'what ifs.'

01-05-17

Took my grandsons to lunch, the library and to the beach. I'm gonna miss them when they go back home. Too bad we had to be together for circumstances of death. But I thank God they're with me and my lil girl can get herself together.

01-06-17

I'm up. I prayed with the kids. My grandsons will be leaving tomorrow and I'm preparing them with clean clothes. I will get them ready for their mom.

01-07-17

158

The boys just left and I'm a little upset. We all prayed together. It's today I realize life is too short. I think I've learned from this whole thing is not to be angry and hold things in with somebody cause you never know when the last time you gonna see them.

After the boys were gone it was time to write. So, like I said, I gathered the poems, started putting them in order and took my daily evening walks, talking with God. I started remembering sayings like, *"This too shall pass." "To thine own self be true."* And I started figuring out these mantras must be put into practice. And I thought, I must educate myself more. Hell, I forgot where the comma went. I must take classes. That's one thing that stuck with me in the Steve Harvey Challenge. What must I do to make my goals happen and my dreams come true?

01-19-17

Wow. It's Day 19 of the challenge. I need to be relieving some stress. My life can't be all about work and writing. I must do something to relieve my stress. So I bought me a crossword puzzle. Since I had my strokes, I had to reprogram my mind on punctuation, spelling and grammar. I pray every day that my memory gets better. And I'm reading and definitely writing better. Almost better than I used to. With some personal events that had taken place since January 1st, the financial part ends tomorrow as planned. I love you my little G' Angel. Joel you have made my life meaningful. And every day I get a little stronger.

01-22-17

Just awoke and I'm smiling. Good morning JoJo. Grandma got your poem. Today I will finish it up the masterpiece, sticking to my resolution. Welcome to heaven grandson.

Dear God,
I feel it coming on. Give me the words that I must write as I <u>*Listen To The Wind*</u>.

As I felt the wind blow across my face and through my hair, it whistled with words. I knew then God was trying to tell me something. As I closed my eyes it reminded me of that day I wrote <u>In A Heartbeat</u>. It was then that I began once again one with God. The oneness I experienced that day gave me a confidence within myself like no other. That day I felt God's power. To try to explain this, there's really no words to describe the supernatural feeling that I felt deep inside me. All I knew at this moment, it was the power of God. And that's really, really all I have to say about that!

Listen to the Wind

Listening to the wind
As it blows thru my ears.
I have heard the sound
for many years.

Listening to the wind
Sounding like thunder.
In a sea shell ... the wind?
Where does it come from?
Who makes it?
I ponder - I wonder.

Listening to the wind,
  As it drys my tears
     Wisked away all my fears.
And takes away my pain of yesterday
makes me wanna pray,
  Makes me wanna
     Thank God,
        for today.

By Netanis L.

As my story draws to an end of my first book and where it began, I didn't let nothing stop me or get in my way. *Perseverance* is my key to my success of never giving up *no matter what.* Like the time in July on the 4th, the Red Cross was called in to a fire that started in our apartment. And in the middle of the floor of that fire, was my handwritten introduction to the book to that was consumed in water, soot, and insulation that fell from the ceiling. It looked like it had been tarred and feathered with all the debris from the sudden surprised fire. Four apartments got affected. In that same year, Hurricane Irma would follow with more devastating circumstances. I got confused a little bit and things were out of order but I just went to God and my prayers continued to be answered, which made me think of the verse: ***Isaiah 54:17 NKJV No weapon that is formed against thee shall prosper;*** Only by none the less, I say by the grace of God I have survived all my trials and bats with death as it is written in the fourth book of the Torah in ***Deuteronomy 20:4 NLT For the Lord your God is going with you! He will fight for you against your enemies, and He will give you victory***. With this verse I knew I was well on my way to recover and take back what the adversary stole from me and then some. With Jesus on my side I did not lose.

James 4:7 (NIV)- So humble yourselves before God. Resist the devil, and he will flee from you

Ephesians 6 (NIV) - Put on the full armor of God, so that you can take your stand against the devil's schemes.

Matthew 6: 13 (NIV) - And lead us not into temptation, but deliver us from the evil one.

This is how I fight my battles by just remembering these verses on a daily basis and saying it aloud, as if to speak it to the devil in times of trials and confusion. I rebuke him immediately and turn back to my father, gazing into the heavens above. I seek His comfort and His refuge. For I long to feel safe in His arms and His love for me keeps my desire of my fire in my heart burning and yearning for Him. I know one day; I'll be where He is. As for my Joel, I am very thankful to God for him. What an impact this little baby made on my life in the short time of 33 months that he was here. I always did call him my little baby Jesus. It was he that brought me back to Christ. Just looking in his eyes I could see God. I could feel the Lord's presence. The way I felt, my words are indescribable. It was like for every month he was here, it stood for every year Jesus lived. The impact this baby, my grandson made on my life was supernatural of how I was delivered from evil by a little innocent child that only stayed a little while but he stayed long enough to influence myself to return back to Jesus and not give up. With this, I try to help others with my story, my proof of how He saved me from a reckless way of living... a wretched soul like me...amazing grace

Finally, in August 2017, Joel's autopsy report came in the mail. It took them so long to get the results to us. I asked the coroner to send them directly to me and not my daughter. She was in no shape to handle this news. He was diagnosed with congenital brain cancer. When I called the doctor I asked him this question, *"Why didn't we see this in the C-scans on the east coast, the west coast and Central Florida?"* The doctors told us there was nothing to worry about. The coroner explained to me that with this kind of brain cancer in infants, you can't see it until an autopsy is performed. He also told me there was nothing we could have really done about it. He also told me that his body was going to slowly get weaker and death was eventually inevitable. So, with this information, I went straight to God for answers.

And He let me know by the Bible verse that He knew the circumstances of Joel in so many words, **"I knew you before I formed you in your mother's womb. Before you were born ..."***Jeremiah 1:5 NLT* From different people, doctors and clergy, and other friends I came to an understanding that *this was the way it was supposed to be. We weren't supposed to know.* When I think back now, if I would have known that no matter what I did or we all did, he was gonna die, that probably would have killed me. Not that I would have used drugs again but I think I would have given up. Often, I wish that God would have taken me in exchange for Joel. But I know today, I have to remember again that's not how God works. He doesn't trade one soul for another.

On March 31, 2018, we had Joel's funeral/memorial/4th birthday celebration/ Easter all in one. In the conclusion of <u>Broken Wings</u>, I give you

Perfect Wings, Tailor Made.
On Golden Wings
   My grandson you
         Soar-
High in the sky,
   Where the lions roar -

Is a baby which I adore,
     Made so perfect now -
       I must say this,
         And something more.
           He has no more,
             "Broken wings"
               Anymore.
                 Netanis Lopez

And look how God works: **Matthew 20:16 NIV "So the last will be first, and the first will be last.**

See Joel never could keep up with his cousins. And he beat them all. He won that race. He made it home first. Another verse that got me through my heartache is **Revelations 21:4 ESV...He will wipe away all tears from their eyes, and there will be no more death, sorrow, crying or pain. All that has gone forever.**

I took his death really hard inside. I went to God and I accepted the fact that my grandson was with Jesus, having a perfect life. And with that, *"I am well with my soul."* It took me back to the verse:

Matthew 5:4 NRSV "Blessed are those who mourn, for they will be comforted." I knew that Jesus was there with me, he never left my side. Up until this day that I finish this book, he is still with me, guiding me through it all.

JESUS
Offers
Everlastin
Life

To help me ease my mind, I had to come to realize the positivity of his name Joel and let it stand for something of Jesus. So I put these words together with his name. To me this is the *truth* because there is everlasting life after death. I believe this is the just a realm we pass through to get to the next life. I feel in my heart the next kingdom is Heaven, as Joel sits *at the right hand side of the rite of the site* of Jesus on the throne.

I take care of my health today. And that's what we're supposed to do anyway. In Corinthians it says: *Or do you not know that your body is a temple of the Holy Spirit within you, whom you have from God? You are not your own. 1 Corinthians 6:19 ESV:* I remember my therapist telling me in treatment, *"Addicts want praise for things they should be doing anyway."* Boy, she was so right about a lot of things. It's today that I take care of my health. I make my doctors' appointments. I stay physically, mentally and spiritually fit. I may not go to church every Sunday but that doesn't mean I forget about God. I keep up with my maintenance by attending recovery meetings on a weekly basis. One of the ways I remain humble is by taking the bus because I never want to forget where I came from. I try to share the message of Christ whenever somebody starts talking to me and starts sharing their story. I tell of what Christ is done for me. My story always seems to amaze others and they always want to hear more. I speak of my book and if I have an extra one on me, which I usually do, I offer it to them. I guess you could say I'm *farming*, planting seeds.

Only God knows what He has in store for me and I continue to stick in there with the winners and when I'm wrong, I admit it. Life hasn't always been easy for me but it gets better each day and I keep doing the next right thing and the next right thing automatically happens after that. And then I do my part, it repeats, so on and so on. I stay in the solution and not the problem by staying connected. I keep it simple by praying about everything and worrying about nothing. I talk to my sponsors and my support group. I keep swimming and swimming and learning and learning. Recovering more, day by day. They say we never fully recover all the way. If we did that, we would all be perfect. There's always something to learn every day. I try to just stay open, teachable and 'spongy,' soaking up all the knowledge by taking notes because I be ready to learn something new. *"When the student is ready, the teacher will appear." Buddha Shakyamuni.* I still keep that in my head and when those light bulbs click on in my mind, I get this natural high of wisdom. With this feeling in my gut of intuition is when the moment comes that I've learned something new. In this high that I get, no drug or any physical action or intimacy can touch... There's no comparison. I smile because I know it's God's light shining in me which takes me to the bible verse: *For He who is in you is greater than he who is in the world."—1 John 4:4, GMG (goodmorninggirls.org)*

Life just seems to get a little easier some days. And I still have a few bad days but the good definitely outweigh the bad. I still ask myself this question. *If I had to change a single thing in my life, what would it be, what year and why?* I would have to say, *"Today it would be "NOTHING!"* Because without going through what I went through all these years, starting with that little baby in the highchair, I wouldn't be who I am today and you certainly wouldn't be reading this book. I thank God today for all that I went through. Having the three strokes, it's like God wiped my mind clean. For my mind was like an automatic road map. I didn't forget about anything. I knew where all the drug holes were at. He installed me with His own GPS, which stands for Grace's Protection Service. At least in my mind. Lol. *Hebrews 10:17 MSG He concludes; I'll forever wipe the slate clean of their sins.* I 'll say Jesus wiped my slate clean for that is a understatement. Not only did He remove my desire to use drugs those strokes I had erased the memory of all the psych meds I was on, however the reasons 'why' I was on them is the material contained in this book. I sure had enough stories to write about and then some.

I thank Him for the good times and I praise Him for the bad times like it says in **1 Thessalonians 5:18 In everything give thanks; for this is the will of God in Christ Jesus for you.** Just because each bad time, there was a great lesson to be learned. Not only has that make me stronger and wiser but I'm able to help other people and other women. I can relate and empathize with just about anything. Or I know someone that can. I know now why God chose me. I feel it`s because I am one of His favorites and one of His strongest warriors and He saves me for His toughest battles. During all the trials that I have been through the most valuable lesson that stays with me the most is *forgiveness.* Before I could forgive anyone else, I had to learn to forgive myself. Resentments, oh boy held one for over four decades. My how it poisoned my soul and devoured my spirit. I vowed to God and to myself that I will never be a victim of my past again. I will use what I have been through to help another. It is today I speak out, *"I am a survivor of my consequences of circumstances as the results from my past."*

Not the end………..

After-word

"And now in age I bud again,
After so many deaths I live and write." ~ George Herbert

-

This year, 2018, is almost to an end. But it's just the beginning for me. I got married again this year to a wonderful, perfect, beautiful, amazing man. Out of all the struggles that I've been through He knows about them all. He has always helped me through them, I just didn't know it. You might know Him too. I talk about Him a lot. His name, *Jesus Christ.* And you may wonder why I love him like I do, let this book be the proof. He is the truth, the way, and the light of my life. He saved me from myself and others when nobody else was there for me, He became the source of my strength. All I can say is, *"God, you even blocked Satan from taking my life. For you Lord have restored me and given me a clean heart."* Everything you have read that I've been through does not compare to what Jesus suffered through. I don't know half the time how I made it through, how I got words to write with and how I came across the right friends to help me just where I needed it the most. For it is written in the WORD ***"…God, who makes everything work together, will work you into his most excellent harmonies." Philippians 4:9 MSG.*** For one most important aspect of this whole book was that God *orchestrated* it all. All I can say is: ***Be still, and know that I am God Psalm 46:10 KJB.*** It still is one of my favorite verses to this day. One of my prayers in my journal when I was writing this book:

Dear God,
With you, I am kept. Wiping the tears, I wept, continually holding me while I slept. I can't wait to see Your face. As I express my feelings to what I am feeling… The wind blows gently, letting me know God is in this place. I just want to give thanks to you Lord for giving me the courage to write this book, as I have put my blood, sweat and tears in it. I thank you for everything you are getting ready to do. May this book inspire, touch, and change everyone who comes across it.
In the name of the Father, Son, and Holy Spirit. Amen.

For the Scriptures say, ***"'As surely as I live,' says the LORD, every knee will bend to me, and every tongue will confess and give praise to God.'" Romans 14:11 NLT*** After all of this and all I've been through, you ain't gotta tell me twice for ***Romans 8:38-39 NIV*** says ***For I am convinced that neither death nor life, neither angels nor demons, neither present nor future, nor height nor depth, not anything else in all creation, will be able to separate me from the love of God that is in Jesus Christ our Lord.*** And that's all I have to say about that!

As my first book draws to its conclusion, you can look forward to my other books that I have already been writing but not completed. For I really didn't know how this book would end and I had to put this out first, so you could understand the rest of my books and stories in them to come. For I truly believe it isn't over, until God says it is. For He has always had the last word in my life when it came to the judges, the doctors and surgeons, and between giving me life or death. Scriptures say give all the glory to God. I praise Him and I am so thankful He used me as His vessel to get His message across of how He saves. *To God be the glory*, my last words I say, as God promised, ***"Behold, I am coming soon" Revelation 22:12 ESV*** And as I have read in other bibles, "Jesus is coming back*; quickly, suddenly, unexpectedly."* Not is definitely not the end for me, it's just the beginning. Thank you for reading my book, my testimony on how God has saved me through His son Jesus Christ. May the Lord, The Prince of Peace be with you all.

Amen.

Back Cover Story

The day I picked my grandsons up from St. Mary's hospital from West Palm Beach we all said our goodbyes to Joel. I promised the boys that I would take them to the beach tomorrow and you know kids don't forget. That day January 5, 2017, at the beach, a seagull with a head full of black feathers soared high above us. While the boys played in the sand, this bird landed beside me while sitting on the blanket. A sense of relief came over me. The thought occurred to me that I was not alone. It was then that I instantly grabbed my phone. As if the bird knew, I was going to take a picture, he spread its wings and maintained its balanced as he floated just above my head. Me, being so nervous and anxious to capture this moment before he flew away again, I hurriedly snapped the picture.

I took a perfect snapshot, only God could make this picture-perfect moment happen at our time of deep, deep sorrow. I felt the presence of Joel and I called his brothers. It was then the bird hovered over them. They pointed and said, *"Ooh Grandma, it's Joel! He's with us!"* And I agreed. *"Yes he is boys. Yes, he is. He's with Jesus now."*

Little did we know at the time, nine months later, this would be the bird that would be on his urn, a replica with the same wing span. This was not planned it was God that orchestrated this. No one could have known this of this bird that spread its wings like that but the Almighty Healer.

This began my journey and my determination to write this book. I didn't know at the time this would be on my back cover. God transformed it like that. The lower picture of myself was December 1, 2016, when I first started *The Challenge*. I took the picture in the local library when I was thinking about how I was going to get this book started. I was thinking in the picture and the patron in the library took the picture. I smiled as I thought. *Hmmm I thought. This is very interesting. I can't believe I'm doing this. It's finally happening.* Looking around at all the books gave me inspiration that I can write a book too. This was my sanctuary. This was my peace. It does exactly what the beach has always done for me. Now it was time to do God's work. I didn't know how. But He did. That day holding the red pen in my hand (to correct mistakes) represented how I write by the blood of Jesus. Because like Him, I get to see the mistakes I make and correct them. **Jeremiah 33:3 ASV Call unto me, and I will answer thee, and will show thee great things, and difficult, which thou knowest not.** I anticipate the great things that He has yet to show me like it says in His word.

I stayed at the library that day until it closed and I took the last bus back home. I began to thank Him for what He was about ready to do in my life and for the people that would be sent my way that I would soon help. For my trial and tribulations were not in vain, they were not for nothing. I must share my story and tell of the miracles that God performed in my life. And He's still doing it to this day. If you're reading this book, you're one of them.

<u>Look For Future Books By Netanis Lopez</u>

A book of grief, stages of grief, poems, and short stories

A collection of poems about mental illness: anxiety, - depression, and other emotions from different viewpoints from different hearts.
– With Dawn Callihan & others

A devotional of real life from His thoughts to mine.

SPECIAL MENTIONS

Cape Coral Library: Magda & Jeffrey – For all your help and understanding.
Joe and Jenna – Physical Therapist
My two daughters – sketches and words
My baby boy – For all his support in believing in me.
Florida Heart Associates: Jeffrey H. Rosen, MD, FACC – Recognition *"The man upstairs has been looking out for you. You are a miracle. I'm looking at a miracle."*
Kairos Outside: I was a guest on weekend #18 and served on the team, weekend #20, #21. A prison ministry designed for women and the children of the men incarcerated and the families of loved ones that are affected and the sentence they serve on the outside.
ITJ – Into the Jordan, Ministry for human trafficking and exploited women survivors.
Bianca Russell: Front cover artist/painter – "The First Joel"
Mike Morgan, PhD: Professor of writing & teachings. - "If it wasn't for you, I wouldn't know where the comma went; *Are we eating at Grandma's or are we eating Grandmas'?"*
Drug Abuse Foundation (DAF), Delray Beach, FL
Joseph G. Ballard – Founder of "The Window Buddy"
Life Care – Lillian Easterly – Smith, BCPC - Help – Hope – Healing
(Counselor & Pastor) www.lifecarechristiancenter.org
Grace Church – All campuses Lead Pastor Jorge Acevedo and his team of pastors
Christy's Cause- works to eradicate the exploitation of children and women of sex and human trafficking / christy@christyscause.com
Frederick S -For use of computer in the caveman room, for taking care of me, and being my #1 son
One Purse founder, Heather Case

FUTURE FOUNDATION GOAL

One day my dream is to start a foundation of red flag alerts for mothers and families of developmental delayed babies. It is my hope that more research be done so that we can find out more information through more image testing and specialized blood work. More education is needed ahead of time at an early age where babies have a better chance of surviving. Maybe other mothers and families won't have to go through false hope by doctors saying, *"Don't worry; He'll grow out of it; We don't see any grey areas."* All along we didn't know there was nothing to ever be done because they didn't know enough about it.

Celebrate Recovery 12 Steps and Biblical Comparisons

1. We admitted we were powerless over our addictions and compulsive behaviors, that our lives had become unmanageable.
"I know that nothing good lives in me, that is, in my sinful nature. For I have the desire to do what is good, but I cannot carry it out." Romans 7:18

2. We came to believe that a power greater than ourselves could restore us to sanity.
"For it is God who works in you to will and to act according to his good purpose." Philippians 2:13

3. We made a decision to turn our lives and our wills over to the care of God.
"Therefore, I urge you, brothers, in view of God's mercy, to offer your bodies as living sacrifices, holy and pleasing to God - this is your spiritual act of worship." Romans 12:1

4. We made a searching and fearless moral inventory of ourselves.
"Let us examine our ways and test them, and let us return to the Lord." Lamentations 3:40

5. We admitted to God, to ourselves, and to another human being the exact nature of our wrongs.
"Therefore confess your sins to each other and pray for each other so that you may be healed." James 5:16

6. We were entirely ready to have God remove all these defects of character.
"Humble yourselves before the Lord, and he will lift you up." James 4:10

7. We humbly asked Him to remove all our shortcomings.
"If we confess our sins, he is faithful and will forgive us our sins and purify us from all unrighteousness." 1 John 1:9

8. We made a list of all persons we had harmed and became willing to make amends to them all.
"Do to others as you would have them do to you." Luke 6:31

9. We made direct amends to such people whenever possible, except when to do so would injure them or others.
"Therefore, if you are offering your gift at the altar and there remember that your brother has something against you, leave your gift there in front of the altar. First go and be reconciled to your brother; then come and offer your gift." Matthew 5:23-24

10. We continue to take personal inventory and when we were wrong, promptly admitted it.
"So, if you think you are standing firm, be careful that you don't fall!" 1 Corinthians 10:12

11. We sought through prayer and meditation to improve our conscious contact with God, praying only for knowledge of His will for us, and power to carry that out.
"Let the word of Christ dwell in you richly." Colossians 3:16

12. Having had a spiritual experience as the result of these steps, we try to carry this message to others and practice these principles in all our affairs.
"Brothers, if someone is caught in a sin, you who are spiritual should restore them gently. But watch yourself, or you also may be tempted." Galatians 6:1

Life Verses to Remember

Psalm 119:105 (KJV) "Thy word is a lamp unto my feet, and a light unto my path."

John 3:16 (KJV) "For God so loved the world, that he gave his only begotten Son, that whosoever believeth in him should not perish, but have everlasting life."

Mathew 6:34 (NIV) "Therefore do not worry about tomorrow, for tomorrow will worry about itself. Each day has enough trouble of its own."

Romans 8:31 (NLT) "What shall we say about such wonderful things as these? If God is for us, who can ever be against us?"

Notes